TRAIN AND DEVELOP YOUR STAFF

A do-it-yourself guide for managers

TRAIN AND DEVELOP YOUR STAFF

A do-it-yourself guide for managers

Alan George

Gower

Published by
Gower Publishing Limited
Gower House
Croft Road
Aldershot
Hampshire GU11 3HR
England

Gower
Old Post Road
Brookfield
Vermont 05036
USA

British Library Cataloguing in Publication Data
George, Alan
Train and Develop Your Staff. A do-it-yourself guide for managers
    1. Employees – Training of
    I. Title
    658.3'124'04

    ISBN 0 566 07840 6

Library of Congress Cataloging-in-Publication Data
George, Alan, 1938–
    Train and develop your staff: a do-it-yourself guide for managers/
    Alan George.
        p. cm.
    Includes index.
    ISBN 0–566–07840–6
    1. Employees–Training of.   2. Employees–Training of–Planning.
3. Organizational learning.   I. Title
    HF5549.5.T7G397   1997
    658.3'124–DC21   97–11021
                                                           CIP

Phototypeset in Palatino by Intype London Ltd and printed
in Great Britain at the University Press, Cambridge.

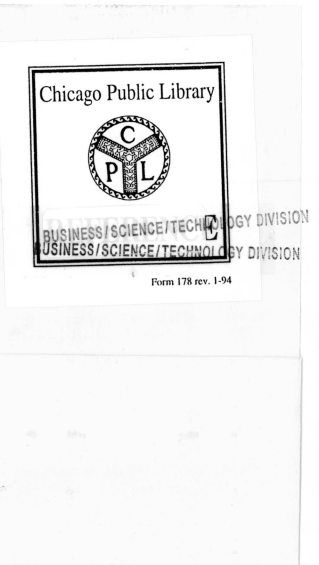

Contents

List of figures and tables

Figures

Tables

Preface

Who is this book for? You are likely to be a manager or supervisor with an interest in improving the performance of your staff. You hope to do this by helping train them and encouraging them to develop new competences. You may also aspire to do more than this: you may want to shift the culture of the work group you manage so that they regard learning in the workplace as a normal and everyday thing to be doing.

You may work in an organization which has its own training and development staff, in which case the book will show you ways of complementing what they can provide and obtaining more value from the courses and workshops they offer.

In smaller organizations you will not have in-house help of this kind and you should find the ideas and techniques you will be reading about give you confidence to develop your own staff as part of your normal management responsibilities.

You may be a trainer who has seen the importance of involving line managers more directly in the development of their own staff. You might choose to ask those who show interest to work through the book section by section, using it as the basis for an action learning set.

The book contains practical help in planning and implementing a wide range of training and development activities. It explains the basic techniques that trainers have developed to help people learn. It also encourages you to reflect on your own day-to-day interactions with your staff and assess to what extent you can spot and develop learning opportunities appropriate to their needs, as well as those of the organization.

It is arranged in 14 chapters, each of which starts with a clear statement of aim and objectives. At the conclusion of each chapter you will find annotated reading lists to support each topic. The early chapters provide a general framework for thinking about learning and helping people learn in the workplace. The main body of the book takes you step by step through the process of planning and providing learning opportunities at work, whether through traditional training workshops or through the many events that you as a manager can use to help develop your staff.

You are offered help in planning to run your own training events and you are encouraged to involve your staff in ensuring that agreed objectives are reached. There is guidance on using open learning as an alternative means of training. The book concludes with three chapters which will help you measure the progress you are making, as a work group or a company, towards becoming a learning organization. You can identify how to develop a more strategic approach to the process of helping people learn.

Writing this book has given me the opportunity to reflect on 15 years of work on training and development projects for many different organizations. Before that I worked with students, both young and old, and I have no doubt that the excitement I still feel when individuals and groups engage in intense learning stems from there.

Tapping the energy and enthusiasm of pupils and students can lead to remarkable outcomes. I think of the group of student architects who in one week designed and produced a solar-heated inflatable pool cover for a nursery school. I remember the commitment and rapid learning curve of a group of staff at Philips who worked with me to produce their own short training video. There are also many more routine examples of steady growth and change, often in the face of difficulties, where individuals broke free from low self-esteem and under-achievement and began to realize just what might be possible. Sadly, too, there have been moments when I did not have the wit or the courage to grasp the opportunity to find learning in sometimes difficult encounters and experiences.

Increasingly, I have come to see that, unless managers assume the role and responsibilities of being staff developers, most of what trainers and training courses can provide may in the longer term be wasted. You and your staff share a commitment to improving performance. Your personal commitment may on occasions exceed theirs, but it is this concern about performance which provides the best trigger for assessing learning needs. The book will help you to do this systematically and it will also help you develop your skills in meeting learning needs through a wide range of imaginative and effective solutions.

Finding ways to help people learn is not a selfless process; in doing it you increase your own capacity to learn and you will make the job of being a manager richer and more rewarding.

Alan George
Calibre Learning Ltd

Acknowledgements

First I would like to acknowledge my wife, Bren, for her support and patience while I wrote this. Eliza, my youngest daughter, should be thanked for the same forbearance.

All my colleagues at Calibre share some credit for the fact that our work has resulted in this book. So my thanks to Jan Fielden and Calibre associate, Steve Voyce, who read and commented on drafts, and to Kathy Burgoyne, Rosie Cinicolo, Anne Prettyman and Catherine Tominey.

It goes without saying that every new assignment presents new challenges and opportunities, so I have to acknowledge Calibre's clients. If they had not required us to deliver, to collaborate and question ourselves, to refine the solutions and avoid complacency, this book would not have been written.

A.G.

Introduction

The assumption of this book is that you are interested in getting the best out of your workforce. You know what a difference well-motivated and enthusiastic staff can make both to the experience of work as well as to the bottom line. You will yourself have had experience of the way those who have managed you have varied in their capacity to get the best out of you. Two of the most important and challenging tasks managers take on are to give leadership and to release the full potential of those they manage.

So how does training and development fit into this? I assume that you are not considering making a career change from manager to trainer/developer, although if you are, you will be embarking on an interesting journey of discovery. Instead, the book proposes that you need to become increasingly aware of how effectively you as a manager can train and develop your own staff. You will quickly realize as you start to read that my view of training and development is very broad. Apart from training workshops and courses, it includes all the day-to-day development opportunities in the workplace, which you can attune yourself to spot and maximize.

Is the climate right for learning?

There need to be fundamental changes in the way we approach managing which, once they begin to occur, will make learning a natural part of people's working lives. These changes include:

- developing a common sense of purpose and direction, call it a mission statement, a vision or what you will, as

1

long as it is clear, inspirational and shared by the whole
organization;

- changing the organizational structure so that more
  decisions are taken in productive work groups rather than
  at the centre;
- responding to customer needs more directly and effectively;
- opening up communications and sharing information
  more widely;
- discussing and agreeing standards of performance and
  giving people more responsibility for meeting them;
- encouraging people to take decisions about the best way
  to do their jobs;
- rewarding creativity;
- enriching work experience by agreeing more challenging
  objectives;
- using mistakes and problems as an opportunity to learn
  to do better.

How does your organization measure up?

The changes described above can be achieved, provided that
you and other managers have the leadership and vision to
grasp them. The rate and direction of change is a product of
how flexible and responsive your organization and its people
are, and how fast the market is changing around you.

What is certain is that if you are not expecting to have to
change, the world will change around you, and increasingly
rapidly. We can either learn from change, sometimes pain-
fully, or we can dig in and hope it may go away; the latter
option, however, is always terminal. The capacity to learn
from all the messages and experiences that come from outside
and within the organization is one of your prime skills as a
manager. If it is important that you are thinking ahead and
anticipating what to do next, you will be greatly helped if
your own work group learns to behave similarly with regard
to their areas of responsibility.

You may have heard people refer to the 'learning organization'. Peter Senge, the American author of the influential
book, *The Fifth Discipline*, writes: 'As the world becomes more

interconnected and business becomes more complex and dynamic, work must become more "learningful".'
A learning organization will be enacting the sort of changes described above. Senior management will need to be open to learn from many sources; however, one of the most important of these is to learn from what is happening in the workforce. No one has a monopoly on knowing how best to meet challenges and solve problems. Organizations which waste learning are structured and run by senior management who think they have learnt all that they need to know. They in turn may actively discourage too much learning elsewhere, as it may be threatening to them. Whatever new knowledge, skills and enthusiasm recruits bring to the job, they quickly abandon or repackage, so that only the bits that the organization is equipped to recognize get used.

Given the complexity of organizations, there will be elements of using and ignoring learning going on continuously around you. I hope that the balance is in favour of using learning. If your whole organization is stuck or, worse still, denying the need to learn, you will encounter resistance from other managers as and when you try to make the most of your work group's potential. You should recognize and be prepared for this and seek some support from like-minded managers within or outside the organization. Unless you have it in mind to be the sacrificial lamb, think twice about taking on the whole organization from a position part-way down the hierarchy. Someone in senior management probably thinks the way you do. Seek them out and try to explain what you would like to achieve with your work group and talk through why you feel the organization is set up to make it difficult to achieve.

How ready is your work group to make positive use of learning?

What evidence can you produce to suggest that the staff in your department, section or work group are receptive to the idea of recognizing and using learning at work? Run through the following checklist to see how they rate using the following rating scale: Never = 1; Rarely = 2; Sometimes = 3; Often = 4; Always = 5. There will always be some variation across the group of course; base your answers on the behaviour of the majority.

Staff contribute ideas and suggestions about how to do the work more effectively. □

They are prepared to talk openly with you about their successes and failures. □

They support members of the group who need help to work better. □

They share responsibility for the induction of new members. □

They demonstrate a commitment to ensuring equal opportunity to learn for all members of the work group. □

They approach staff appraisal in a positive frame of mind. □
(If you do not have a formal scheme, you will find more on this in Chapter 12, 'Assessing learning outcomes'.)

They identify training opportunities and come to you for your support. □

After they have attended a training event or completed a course, they discuss with you how to use what they have learnt. □

They show that they regard other parts of the organization as internal customers, not competitors or obstacles. □

They demonstrate an understanding of, and a commitment to, the overall mission of the organization. □

You will no doubt have guessed that what you are measuring in this activity is as much to do with the way you manage your staff as with their readiness to learn. You set the values and the standards for your work group. You create some possibilities or close down others. Before reviewing what rating you have made in this activity, reflect on the length of experience you and your work group have had together. You may, for example, have inherited a group where little attention has been given to training and development, whether in terms of investment in courses and workshops or in basic processes such as staff appraisal and the drawing up of development plans. You yourself may have been finding your feet as a manager and be now more ready and confident to plan the development of your staff. So, with these factors in mind, how did you score in the activity?

If you have scored 10–25, you need to take this starting position into account and not expect miracles overnight. On the other hand, there is much to be gained from creating a new environment at work. What you will learn from using this book should provide you with the tools for the job.

If you scored in the 25–45 range, you are already gathering useful experience which should help consolidate your role as a manager. Look at any of the ten areas listed in the activity where you have scored below 3. Ask yourself why this is so, and what you can start doing to improve the situation.

If you scored above 45, congratulations; you should be seeing the benefits of training and development in the improved performance of your work group. As you read this book, look for ways that you can go on improving; check that you are not missing important opportunities to maximize the potential of your staff.

You cannot learn on behalf of other people, nor compel them to learn. They need the motivation but they also need the learning environment to support their wish to learn. You are part of that environment. You as a manager can create possibilities and provide resources and encouragement. You can create expectations and set standards which make it more likely that people will experience work as an opportunity to learn.

How this book will help you train and develop your staff

To help you plan how to use this book, here is an overview of its contents.

In Chapter 1, 'How people learn at work', you can identify a number of factors which contribute to effective learning. An important theory about learning from experience is explained. Mistakes can also provide learning opportunities.

In Chapter 2, 'Helping people learn at work', you can read more about the different ways managers support learning. You can also learn more about how adults learn and how we all have our own preferred ways of learning. In the work-place, experience plays a key role, but there is also a place for guided reflection and learning more about the theories, techniques and approaches that help make sense of experience.

In Chapter 3, 'Improving performance', you will be shown how to identify those aspects of your staff's performance which need to be improved by changes in the way you manage them and the environment in which they work. Start here rather than plunge straight into training and develop-ment activities, which in some situations may not solve the problem. The overriding aim is to ensure that you manage to get the best out of your work group, so if you can improve the chances of this happening by changes to the circumstances of the job, you should address this first. In this chapter you will consider the common causes of under-performance and plan ways of addressing them.

Chapter 4, 'Learning needs and how to analyse them', offers you a systematic way of finding out what learning needs your work group has and planning how to meet them. You will find out how to distinguish between the processes of identifying and analysing learning needs. You will be encouraged to base your identification of learning needs on evidence gathered in the workplace. Any analysis you do must lead on to practical solutions and you will be given some guidance on this.

Chapter 5, 'Choosing training events', will help you choose, from the wide range of courses and workshops on offer, those that meet your needs and criteria. The first step is to find out what is available and there are some suggestions about how to do this. You will acquire some background information on accreditation and NVQs. The chapter also deals with using in-house or external providers and how to choose and brief a trainer.

In Chapter 6, 'Getting the best out of training events', you will learn how to plan staff attendance at training events, so that they learn in a purposeful way. This means preparing them for the selected course or workshop, by checking their expectations and encouraging them to do any pre-course work. You will also need to follow up the event by checking on their views, assessing what they learned and helping ensure that it is used to full advantage in the workplace.

In Chapter 7, 'Developing your staff as they work', you will find out how to help your staff use the day-to-day experience of work as a means of developing their effectiveness. You can plan what questions you need to ask yourself and an individual member of staff as you assign, manage and evaluate day-to-day work, so that the process generates learning outcomes. You will also make some choices about which methods you can use with your own staff. These include acting up, Action Learning, coaching, delegation, mentoring, project work and work shadowing.

Chapter 8, 'Training and development opportunities outside the workplace', describes a range of off-the-job opportunities and helps you assess their relevance to your work situation. These include away days, outdoor learning, community action, secondments, study visits, exhibitions and exchanges.

Chapter 9, 'Using open learning', will help you make an informed decision on whether to use this way of delivering learning. If you do decide to do so, you will be able to plan how best to introduce and develop it as part of your training and development strategy. You will assess the benefits and costs of open learning. Since materials are the essential medium for this type of training, you will consider how to track them down and evaluate their usefulness. Open learning is still new to some organizations, so you need to think about the best ways to introduce it in yours.

In Chapter 10, 'Planning a training event', you can work through the process of running your own training event. You need first to be sure that running a training event is the best course of action, bearing in mind all the other options you have worked on in earlier chapters. Everyone feels apprehensive about delivering events like this, but careful planning and a preparedness to be flexible in delivery can give you the necessary confidence. The chapter provides an example of how to plan an event.

In Chapter 11, 'Delivering a training event', you can build on the planning process and consider a range of training methods that are likely to ensure the participation and involvement of your staff. There is also practical guidance on using audio-visual resources and setting up the domestic arrangements for training. The chapter concludes with a sample evaluation form that you can adapt for your own needs.

Chapter 12, 'Assessing learning outcomes', deals with ways of assessing what learners achieve, whether through formal training or during work-based learning activities, and planning further developments. Giving and receiving good-quality feedback are both vital if people are to learn from what they have done. This leads on to performance appraisal; if it is well managed it can provide an excellent opportunity for supportive and developmental comment on performance. There are suggestions on the place of peer and upwards appraisal.

In Chapter 13, 'Learning development in your work group', you can review what you are doing to achieve a more organized approach to the management of staff development. What are you doing about the selection and induction of new employees and how can you sustain their enthusiasm once they have settled into the post? Have you got a staff appraisal scheme and are you using it to generate individual and group plans for training and development? You will also find help on drafting learning development policy and procedures.

Chapter 14, 'Learning for change', helps you take stock of the extent to which yours is a learning organization and identify priorities for further development. You can compare your organization with a range of others with progressively sophisticated approaches to training and development. You can also consider some key techniques for introducing change and ensuring that it gains support.

The book concludes with a learning development planner. You will consider what you need to be doing to improve your own management skills as a staff developer. To help you do this, you may decide to record, as you read each chapter, learning points that are relevant to you. Use these in completing a SWOT analysis on your situation. You will conclude by drawing up your own plans to create a better learning environment in your work group.

Summary

In this introductory chapter you have begun to identify how well learning is recognized and used in your organization and within the group of staff that you manage. Some environments are hospitable to learning; there is a positive will to share and learn and an avoidance of blaming and playing safe. If you have had the good fortune to work in a positive learning environment you will easily recognize where this book is starting from. If at the moment your experience is not so positive, use the ideas in this book to start making a change.

Reading on

Handy, C., (1989), *The Age of Unreason*, London: Business Books. (A thought-provoking modern classic on change and the need to rethink organizations, careers and learning at work.)

Kline, P. and Saunders, B. (1993), *Ten Steps to a Learning*, Arlington: Great Ocean. (A readable way into the mysteries of the learning organization.)

Senge, P.M. (1990), *The Fifth Discipline*, London: Century Business/Random House. (One of the most commonly referred to books on the learning organization, but you will need to read with determination.)

1

How people learn at work

Some people learn confidently and grow into new jobs, while others deliver average performance or lose their sense of direction and fail to make progress. There could be a number of reasons for this. For example, it could be a consequence of the effectiveness of the recruitment and induction process, the match between job demands and the individual's resources or the quality of management support and structure that is provided. Some of these management areas are beyond the scope of this book, but the notion of managers' support for employee development is at the centre of it. As a first step you need to understand how people learn at work, or indeed in any setting. What makes for a good learning experience? Then in Chapter 2, 'Helping people learn at work', you can identify your role in helping people learn. You can also sharpen the skills that managers use to great advantage in this process.

The aim of this chapter is to help you to understand better how people learn at work. To achieve this you will be asked to:

- *identify some of the key factors which influence learning;*
- *recognize that everyone has their own preferences as to how they learn.*

These are the topics you will be reading more about:

- *effective learning;*
- *how adults learn;*
- *learning from experience;*
- *learning differences;*
- *using mistakes creatively;*
- *motivation to learn.*

Effective learning

First we can make some basic observations about the conditions for effective learning at any age or for any purpose.
As you read through this list, think of examples from your
own experience as a learner.

1 *Build on what you already know.* Learners need a way of
   relating new learning to old. If the gap is too big, you
   cannot develop a map of new knowledge or have the
   confidence to develop significantly new skills.
2 *Use a variety of methods.* In more formal learning situations we need to experience a change of sensory input
   to stimulate attention. One voice, no matter how attractive, will eventually bore. Some research on lecturing
   suggests that many students' attention span lapses at
   about 15 minutes into the lecture and only revives
   at intervals when the lecturer changes topics or shows a
   slide. Learning is easier and more stimulating when we
   can switch between methods, including reading, listening, viewing, doing and speaking. It is said that you
   remember:
   • 10 per cent of what you hear;
   • 50 per cent of what you hear and see;
   • 90 per cent of what you hear, see and do.
   Speaking, reading and writing are the channels of communication that are preferred for academic teaching and
   assessment in many disciplines. However, we also learn
   from observation and participation in live settings, or by
   proxy through TV, film, video, audio and multimedia.
   We can learn by doing. We can learn through reflection
   and planning. The learning process should be as varied
   and stimulating as the real world on which it is based.
   However, some of the vagaries, complexities and unpre-
   dictability of real life need to be controlled in a learning
   experience, either beforehand by developing a simulation
   of it or afterwards by de-briefing and reflecting on what
   happened.
3 *Be physically comfortable.* If you are tired, too hot, cold,

thirsty, hungry or distracted by noise, you will find the effort of learning too much. There are also good and bad times for certain types of learning; consider, for example, which part of the day is your prime time for thinking and reading. It varies from person to person.

4   *Recognize that feelings affect learning.* How you feel about yourself as a learner is closely linked with how you feel about yourself as a person and an employee.

5   *Recognize that confidence affects competence and vice versa.* Competence boosts confidence. In helping people learn you need to increase their confidence that the chosen learning objectives are within their reach.

6   *Motivation is vital.* If you do not want to learn something or think from the start that you are going to fail, the will to progress will seep away. Appreciating this is so vital to an understanding of how to help people learn that we shall come back to it later in the chapter.

7   *Mistakes can be learning opportunities.* Recognizing mistakes and their causes may provide a number of learning opportunities. Whether or not these opportunities can be grasped and used depends very much on the culture of an organization. If, for example, the first reaction when something goes wrong is to find someone to blame, the only thing that anyone will learn is to cover their back. More positively, a calm and objective discussion of what went wrong may identify faults in working practices, in materials, in quality of service or gaps in staff competence or knowledge. This can then result in planned improvement.

8   *Successes can be learning opportunities.* It is just as important to learn from successes; what aspects of performance were particularly effective and why? How can this improved performance be used as a standard and built into future jobs?

9   *Learning is hard to do in a vacuum.* We need feedback on progress. We all thrive on indications of success; how often we need the pat on the back, and how effusive it has to be, depends on how secure and confident we feel in ourselves. It also depends on how we feel about the

person who makes the judgement and how we rate the criteria they applied to our performance.

10 *Learning needs to be reviewed and reinforced if it is to be retained.* Think how much you can now recall of the subjects you were examined in at school. Think how much you can remember of the last training course you attended. Unless you systematically review and use what you learn, it becomes very difficult to recall.

11 *Engaging the whole person.* It is interesting to note in the list above how much feelings feature. Learning is rarely just an intellectual process; our feelings about learning and the progress we are making in a particular piece of learning are inextricably linked. There often seems to be a great deal at stake in achieving through learning. Think how exasperated you felt the last time that you failed to work out a trick or a test in some party game or pub quiz. The 'failure' is trivial, but if it is observed by a group you may feel more foolish than you need to. The experience of submitting to a driving test is also a powerful reminder of how our confidence can be affected by being assessed.

12 *Left and right brain.* The two sides of the brain process different types of thinking. The left side predominantly handles such activities as intellectual analysis, speech, calculations, reading, writing, complex physical activities, ordering and evaluation. The right-hand side is predominantly associated with creativity, colour, music, emotions, artistic activity, recognition, comprehension, spatial abilities, intuition and facial expressions.

The implication of this is that learning activities which only use predominantly one side of the brain risk being less effective than those that use both. In fact, people who mainly learn through either the left or right side of their brain may find it quite difficult to use the other side when they need to. Perhaps when we say 'I can't draw' or 'I'm no good at maths' we are recognizing this imbalance in the way our learning has developed. Of course such judgements may also be the consequence of conditioning through negative feedback at school or at home.

Experts support the view that training and development is more effective if people learn through a variety of channels and in different modes. That is to say, training should be designed so that people have the opportunity to learn through creativity as well as intellectual analysis, and through thinking, doing and feeling. The choice of approach will be influenced by the learning objectives that need to be met; but too often training events become set in one particular rut.

Training has to lead to practical outcomes. The application of skills or the use of the knowledge is more important than simply knowing or being able.

How adults learn

Adult learning, and vocational learning as a sub-set of it, have been much researched. What does this research tell us that can be useful in understanding how people learn at work? How does adult learning differ from learning as a child? Readiness to learn in adults is mainly linked to developmental tasks that they have to do or choose to do. So as a child you study a wide curriculum at school as a part of the general process of learning about the world and the skills, culture and values that society thinks you need to learn about. The things which you now learn are probably to do with work, or home, or some pastime or interest that you pursue outside work. You choose many of them. Work-related learning projects only really succeed if you have some level of commitment to them because you see them as an important part of your work.

The time perspective for an adult learner changes, too. When you were at school you could say that you learnt things 'on spec'. It had been decided that in order to be educated you needed to know these things for your future well-being, for employment or as the basis for further study.

As an adult, you learn because you need to know how to understand, use, do, process, or handle something now or in the very near future. This probably means that the focus of what you learn shifts from subject – for example, biology, the

English novel or nineteenth-century history – to task. So it is probable that you are reading this book because you are interested in solving the 'task' of developing your staff to their full potential, not because you plan to write exam answers or essays about training. Of course, as a rounded person you still learn for reasons which are not solely utilitarian, but you are the one who chooses how you spend your learning time and you pursue only those things which are personally interesting and/or useful to you.

Unlike children, adults bring accumulated life and job experiences to the process of learning. They have their own values, beliefs, views and opinions. They will therefore have their own different motivations for doing things and will generally have a sense of their individual needs.

Learning from experience

Can people learn just by doing? To some extent we all do this, but it is fairly unsatisfactory. At best, you may recognize a rule or an approach which is obviously working well for you, and turn it into your own to use again in different situations. At worst, you might simply be learning and re-learning the worst way of doing something, or your prejudice or lack of self-esteem may be reinforced by bad experience, leaving you with no other ideas or solutions. What matters is that you have a system for learning from experience in a structured way. Usually this structure comes from a teacher or trainer who gives you comment and feedback and provides theories to explain what happened in some practical situation. For example, in sports training the learner might be practising to hit a golf ball. If they have the benefit of being coached, they can use the feedback the coach gives them to reflect on their posture, grip, swing, force and flow. Through guided practice they can apply this feedback to future games. The experience of being coached also develops the learner's capacity to be more reflective and analytical about their performance in general. As the performance improves, they become more sharply aware of the difference between poor, average and good performance. Assuming they are actually making some improvement, their confidence in what they can now do increases and this contributes to their general sense of being in charge of themselves and their learning.

The American psychologist, David Kolb (Kolb, Rubin and McIntyre, 1974), observed this process of using experience as a part of an experiential learning cycle and developed an approach which has been widely used by trainers and others. It is often described by using a diagram like Figure 1.1.

This learning cycle diagram is intended to show the relationship between experience, reflection, theory and planning. You need to think about what you have done to see whether you could have done it differently or better. This reflection tends to happen inevitably if you are concerned about the way you did something. If you use the learning cycle approach you will consciously practise reflecting on all important pieces of work, whether apparently successful or not.

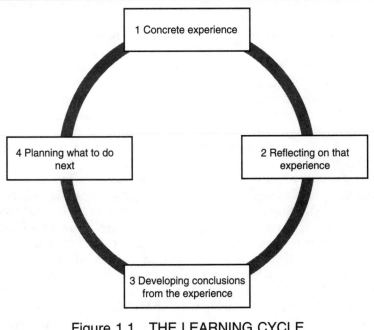

Figure 1.1   THE LEARNING CYCLE

We may start to learn about a new topic or process from a number of different positions around the learning cycle. Which we choose depends in part on our preferred learning style. To take a practical example, imagine that you have just acquired a new computer software package, or a new piece of equipment.
How do you find out how to use it?

1   Do you open it up and try it out (concrete experience)?
2   Do you try it out but then stop and analyse where you are making progress and where you are getting stuck (reflecting on experience)?
3   Having reflected, do you try to work out the rules for using the package more effectively, and at this stage might you read part or all of the manual to confirm your hypotheses (developing conclusions from the experience)?
4   Having reflected, developed your conclusions and drawn on relevant theory, do you plan a practice session to see if it works the way you expect (planning what to do next)?

We really need to work round the whole cycle, perhaps more than once, to internalize new learning. Some people always prefer to try things out first. Then they may reflect on what they did and make some changes. However, this will not seem an attractive solution to everyone and you may have to show some people how to reflect and develop a more theoretical awareness, instead of constantly getting stuck at stage 1 in a series of concrete experiences from which they learn very little.

Reflection alone may provide some answers, but in some situations reflecting may lead to dead ends and the learner may lose motivation because they remain puzzled as to why things worked out the way they did. In this situation either you as their manager or they as the learner need to find some theory or set of reasons which explains causes and effects and which can be used to progress the work, solve the problem or develop the skill.

Having grasped the relevance of the theory or technique, the learner needs to apply it to the task so that they experience confidence in their new skills and resources. In this way they know that they can do this and similar jobs in the future. They have completed the learning cycle and have learned.

Learning differences

As you read about the learning cycle you may have found that you tend to take more naturally to one stage than another. For example, there are those who fight shy of computer manuals and much prefer to open the box and try the package out. They will usually prefer to start at stage 1 of the learning cycle – concrete experience. They probably then reflect and develop their own conclusions and theories about the package and may or may not draw on the information in the manual.

We all show preferences for how we learn, some of which derive from nature and some from nurture. As we grow up we find that some ways of learning things work better for us. The fact that people learn in different ways, not to mention at different speeds, tends to be ignored in many conventional teaching environments. It is probably those who can make the biggest adaptations to compensate for the inflexibility of teaching who succeed best in formal settings. Fortunately, in the type of learning that you can encourage and support as a manager you have the chance to be more flexible and responsive, particularly where you are working with individual members of staff in a coaching role.

Using the four stages of the cycle as a framework, theorists (Honey and Mumford, 1982) have proposed four learning styles. These learning styles are characterized in the following types of behaviour.

1 *Activist.* Activists tend to act first and consider the implications of their actions second. They are always attracted to the opportunity of trying something new and rising to challenges. They are much less interested in seeing things through to a conclusion. They are gregarious, but like to be the centre of attention.

2 *Reflector.* Reflectors prefer to collect all relevant information and analyse it before reaching a decision. They

tend to be cautious and like to draw on the opinions of others before making up their minds. They may appear withdrawn and untouched by what is going on around them.

3 *Theorist.* Theorists feel most at home when they can draw all available theories and observations together and structure them into a logical and linear framework. They tend to be systematic and intolerant of things that cannot be explained logically. They prefer to analyse and be objective rather than deal in subjectivity or ambiguity.

4 *Pragmatist.* Pragmatists prefer to experiment and try things out. They seek out new ideas and like to test them in practice. They find open-ended discussions a waste of time. They are practical and like to solve problems and respond to opportunities by action.

Maybe you recognize dimensions of these styles in your own and others' approach to learning. We are none of us totally and permanently locked into one style. If you are more aware of your preferred learning style, you can understand better why you behave as you do. With this knowledge you can then choose to develop some of the other dimensions which come less naturally.

If you would like to measure more accurately the profile of your learning style, Honey and Mumford (1982) have developed a questionnaire which you can complete and assess for yourself.

Using mistakes creatively

Earlier in this chapter it was argued that we learn by making mistakes, reflecting on them and trying to do things differently and better. We should also try to learn from successes. Our capacity to learn from mistakes will vary depending on a range of factors. Perhaps for many of us it would depend on how public the mistake was, how others reacted to it and what costs were involved. For some people the mistakes that they made at school or at home may have resulted in instant punishment. It is a patient and insightful teacher who can start to unravel a mistake by asking the pupil why they think it happened, what went wrong and how they might work towards the correct solution.

However, in many minor ways throughout the working day we become aware of mistakes that we make, some of them trivial and some more far-reaching. As we do this, we internally adjust and improve our performance. The quality of this internal dialogue and the decisions we make during it are major indicators of our capacity to learn and act more effectively. Do you use this dialogue to reflect negatively on what has gone wrong, maybe taking the blame for it on yourself? Or do you accept responsibility only for what you did wrong and not for what was beyond your power to alter? Most importantly, do you ask yourself what the mistake has taught you? Do you build on and learn from mistakes or collect them like emblems of a more general failure? Reflect on your own experience. Suppose you are producing your first report for a meeting. You struggle with it and are surprised at the difficulties you experience. You know you are going to be very much on show and so you spend a long time refining it. You circulate the report a week beforehand and then present it at the meeting. As you do so you realize that some of it has worked well as a piece of communication. Then someone whose judgement you trust asks you what you meant when you said X on page 4. You wonder how they could still be uncertain about this – they're not slow on the uptake. X is one of the two important concepts you need to communicate. You thought that you had given a perfectly adequate explanation of it on page 1.

If that happened to you, what would you think? Either the person concerned was dozing or distracted, or maybe you have not written your report in a way that communicates as clearly as you hoped. Depending on your confidence, experience or temperament, you will approach your next piece of report writing differently. You have probably learnt from the mistake that you need to practise your writing and presentation skills so that you really do highlight key points.

The capacity to reflect on experience and reach positive conclusions on how to maintain and improve performance is a vital learning skill. In the next chapter you will be given guidance on ways to encourage this to happen in your staff.

Motivation to learn

Significant learning cannot be forced on people at any age, but this is particularly true of adults. They are not susceptible to the threat of detentions or being sent to the head teacher; they choose whether or not to learn. You can probably recall at some time in your own work experience being required to submit to some training event which you did not want to attend. It is usually obvious to a trainer within minutes of the start of a course who is there because they were sent.

Writers on motivation have developed a number of theories to explain the combination of factors that creates in us a readiness to act. Broadly, we either do things because we seek external reward, such as salary, bonuses, admiration and influence, or internal rewards, such as meeting our own goals and targets, a sense of achievement and inner satisfaction. Motivation to learn is rarely to do with solely external or internal rewards. There is usually a blend of the rewards others give us and those which we derive from within. Motivation is also conditioned by past learning experience and the picture we have created of ourselves as learners. You only have to have the confidence knocked out of you once or twice by an insensitive teacher or instructor to leave you feeling that you are no good at learning a particular topic or in a particular way.

As a manager, you will already know that giving rewards in the form of praise and informed feedback can have as powerful an effect on performance as financial rewards. People like to know that their work is appreciated and although pay rises and promotion still remain the most tangible long-term indicators of success, managers need to give regular feedback on performance and praise what is good. As opportunities for promotion and extra pay become harder to find in lean organizations, praise and providing development opportunities may become one of the few ways to motivate staff.

There is no doubt that motivation to learn works in the same way. People may give themselves a pat on the back when they have completed a course or worked through an open learning unit; but most of us like to receive feedback on progress. Find time to take an interest in learners' progress and know enough about what they are doing to give them quality feedback. If you are too busy, delegate this responsibility to a colleague. Without support and feedback, most people's motivation to learn will wither away.

Summary

You have considered the conditions that make for effective learning. These range from building new learning on what you already know, to exploiting the differences between right- and left-brain learning.

Next you identified some of the features which are associated with adult learning. Adults tend to learn because they need to know or do something in the here and now. They also bring accumulated life and job experience which conditions how they learn.

Learning by experience is more than learning by trial and error. You considered a key concept, the experiential learning cycle. This incorporated four stages – concrete experience, reflecting on that experience, developing conclusions from the experience and planning what to do next.

People have preferred ways of learning; you considered the roles of the activist, the reflector, the theorist and the pragmatist.

The chapter concluded with two short sections, one on using mistakes creatively and the last on motivation to learn.

This chapter on learning has just touched on a few of the more important and relevant aspects of the subject. It is an enormous area of study and it continues to grow. In the next chapter you will be invited to use what you have learnt here to ensure that the way you operate as a manager does increase the likelihood that people will learn.

Reading on

Cotton, J. (1995), *The Theory of Learning; An Introduction*, London: Kogan Page. (Offers a useful way into a complex field and is firmly linked to practice.)

Honey, P. and Mumford, A. (1982), *Manual of Learning Styles*. Dr Peter Honey, Ardingly House, 10 Linden Avenue, Maidenhead, Berkshire SL8 6HB. (Use this to find out more about your learning style and those of your staff.)

Kolb, D.A., Rubin, I.M. and McIntyre, J.M. (1974), *Organizational Psychology: A Book of Readings*, 2nd edn, New Jersey: Prentice Hall. (If you want to go back to the source of the learning cycle idea, you will find the key diagram on page 28.)

■ 2

Helping people learn at work

*Building on the ideas in the previous chapter on how people learn,
consider now what you can do as a manager to make it more likely
that they will. You can help people learn in a wide variety of ways,
ranging from demonstration and coaching on the job to arranging
for staff to attend courses or work-shadow a more experienced colleague. This range of methods is described more fully in the
subsequent chapters. However, now you will lay some foundations
by planning how to improve your basic skills in developing your
staff.*

*The aim of this chapter is to help you to understand better what
helps people learn at work and to develop skills in encouraging
learning. To achieve this you will be asked to:*

- *plan to create the circumstances which support learning in the
  workplace;*
- *improve your skills in helping people to learn.*

These are the topics you will be reading more about:

- *your role in helping people learn;*
- *the skills you need to help people learn;*
- *creating a learning environment.*

Your role in helping people learn

You will be aware from your own experience that managers
adopt different approaches when they try to help people

learn. You may have come across managers who did some or all of the following:

1   dropped people in at the deep end and hoped they would cope;
2   fussed around people when they appeared not to be performing well;
3   delegated jobs carelessly and then had to reassign them or take them back when they went wrong;
4   spent time working with a member of staff to get a first-hand assessment of them as a worker and a person;
5   agreed and monitored objectives and made sure that there was sufficient challenge in the job;
6   arranged for people to go on training courses;
7   listened carefully when people exhibited signs of concern about their work;
8   spent time working on a number of development options with their staff;
9   agreed a series of development activities as a consequence of conducting a performance appraisal;
10   recognized that they as the manager may not have been the best person to help and involved another colleague or suggested a mentor.

No prizes for guessing that the first three approaches are not recommended. Option 1 may occasionally work, but might equally well lead to the employee feeling demoralized and deskilled. Options 2 and 3 offer no help to an employee who is trying to improve or learn at work. Approaches 4 to 10 should all contribute to putting staff development firmly on the agenda. They do, though, depend on the manager being organized and sufficiently on top of the job to make the development of his or her staff a priority.

As a manager you will need to identify and use a range of basic interpersonal skills. Many of these are part of your existing repertoire when you deal with employees.

You will also make choices about how to behave which reflect your own management style and the particular needs of each employee in a given situation. In the next section we shall look at these skills and consider how you may use them with your staff.

The skills you need to help people learn

It is worth emphasizing again that the skills needed to help people learn are also by and large those which make for good management in general. By encouraging trust and openness you are creating the opportunity to steer people towards development opportunities at work.

Demonstrate good learning behaviours

One of the most important contributions you can make towards helping people learn is to model learning behaviours yourself. If you are closed to experience and carry on regardless without reflecting on it or learning from it, you will not be much use to those you manage. This proposition may be quite threatening to some managers who would, for example, prefer always to be seen to be right. People learn from making mistakes and that includes managers.

What is suggested here is an opportunity to develop a new relationship with a work group. It will mean being able to admit mistakes or being flexible in changing priorities, provided decisions are based on well-researched information. It will also mean encouraging suggestions and ideas which will lead to more effective work. Managers should be receptive to these from any quarter and in particular from those who have front-line and day-to-day contact with clients and customers.

Show commitment

Show that you believe in the mission of your organization and the part that your work group is playing in fulfilling it. If you do not have a clear understanding of this and a commitment to meeting it, you are in a weak position to shape the development of the group and its members.

Standards which underpin performance also need to be clearly defined and shared with staff. If you do not know what standards you are aiming for, or you do know but have not the commitment and consistency to stick to them, this will be reflected in variable commitment by employees. What they learn from this will be that the wind blows hot and cold and some people can get away with murder while others are urged to try harder.

Being sure of your position as a staff developer is no more than you would expect from effective managers in any of their other functions. However, do not confuse assertiveness, confidence and conviction with inflexibility and doggedness. There is more on the important personal skill of assertiveness in the section on challenge (page 33).

Listen

First, do you make time to listen? Managers who say 'My door is always open' are probably perceived to be people who are too busy to get out of their offices. It can also be inhibiting for some employees to have to enter your territory to talk about something. You need to get out and be available. You may feel you do this and now have the problem of using up too much precious time in what often becomes little more than a social chat. So you also have to learn how to control time spent listening and make sure that you use it for the things that matter.

Think back over the last few weeks and recall how often you spent ten minutes or more with an individual member of staff. What proportion of this time was taken up by your listening? Did you allow space for the person to say all that they wanted? Did you encourage them to be open with you by not jumping to conclusions or criticizing before you had all the facts?

Some of the commonest problems with listening are:

1   only hearing what you want to hear;

2 not giving your full attention to what is being said;
3 accepting what is said at face value;
4 interrupting the speaker and suppressing their desire to talk;
5 giving little or no feedback and leaving the speaker uncertain of what you think.

Reflect on your way of responding to an employee's request to talk. Think of a number of such occasions with different members of staff. Do you, as in examples 1 and 2, use selective attention? You approach the conversation with a mind set which automatically discounts a significant percentage of what this particular employee may say because they always exaggerate/whinge/cover up/pass the buck/gossip (choose the one that fits). Of course you would not respond like this unless there was some past experience to draw on but you may be blinkered by this and miss something important. If they are giving you the usual excuses, maybe you should find ways of shifting the relationship so that it is clear to them that you are interested in what they want to say, not all this posturing. If you are trying to listen to someone at a time when you genuinely should be attending to something much more important, do them the courtesy of re-scheduling the chat, rather than sit there shifting your feet and your gaze. Your body language will give you away.

Example 3 is another form of non-listening. You have to concentrate and do more than just hear to be a good listener. There may be all sorts of clues which need to be followed up by supplementary questions so that you can get to the real facts of the matter. This is particularly the case if the speaker is diffident about self-disclosure as they make the effort to reveal something important about their work and their relations with colleagues.

Some managers cannot shut up; they see conversations with staff as a chance to unfold yet again their vision of the world or the problems that they face in earning their higher salary. Of course you would not fall into this category (example 4), but we all need to develop the skill of not jumping in with our own story. Nodding reassurance and leaving the speaker space to continue will often open up a dialogue at a deeper and more useful level.

Example 5 could happen if you take example 4 too far. Giving no reaction can amount to a form of silent aggression.

Gather information

In talking to staff you often need to be sure that you have the full facts as the speaker sees them. Use open questions to encourage the employee to fill in the gaps in your information. By asking who, where, when, what, why and how, you will discover much more than by asking closed questions which elicit little more than a yes or a no.

This would certainly be a useful approach if you are presented with an account of a problematic situation where something has gone wrong and accusations are being made. However, all work conversations benefit from an initial stage of information gathering. For example, if someone comes with a request for your support or for you to make a decision or agree on some expenditure, you need to explore the facts first.

If you are concerned to know the member of staff better and decide how well they are growing in the job, you would use this technique of gathering information before making an assessment of future training or development needs; this is the main task during the first part of an appraisal interview. You may decide to defer a decision until other people have been contacted or you have had time to reflect and refer to previous records. Recording information during or straight after interviews and conversations is also good practice.

The extent to which you can create an open exchange of information with a member of staff depends on the amount of trust between you, your skill in listening to and using the information given you, and the readiness of the employee to disclose their feelings and wishes.

There is a very useful model which trainers use to illustrate this process (see Figure 2.1). It is called the Johari window (after its American inventors, Joseph Luft and Harry Ingham). It is used to describe disclosure and discovery in a helping

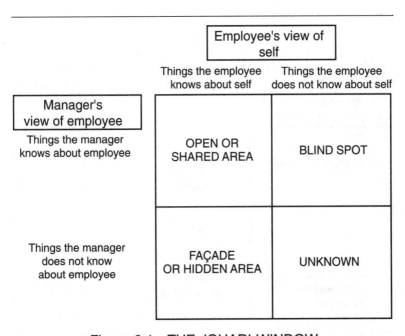

Figure 2.1   THE JOHARI WINDOW

relationship, in this case the relationship between the manager intending to help an employee learn.

The diagram shows four panes of the window. The two on the left, seen from the employee's point of view, have the following significance. The open or shared area is the self-knowledge that the employee is prepared to reveal and discuss with the manager; the façade or hidden area is that which the employee knows about themselves but which they do not wish to share.

The right-hand panes represent those areas which the employee does not know about themselves. The top-right pane, however, represents those things which the manager has seen and knows about the employee – the employee's blind spot. The bottom-right pane represents those aspects of the employee's self which are unknown to both the manager and the employee.

As the relationship develops during the interview or over

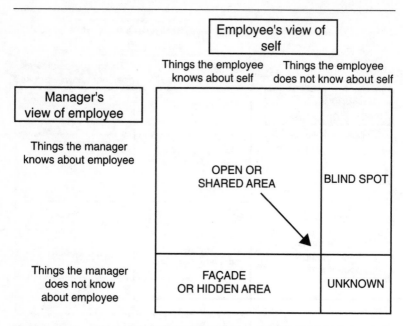

Figure 2.2   THE JOHARI WINDOW: DIRECTION OF THE HELPING RELATIONSHIP

a period of time, the manager hopes to be able to create sufficient trust to encourage the employee to increase the size of the open or shared pane at the expense of the façade or hidden pane. The manager may also be able to move the employee's self-perception on the horizontal axis so that what has been a blind spot to them becomes part of the shared open area. The arrow in this second version of the diagram (Figure 2.2) shows the direction in which this helping relationship should move.

You might choose to refer in your mind to the Johari window next time you experience difficulty in getting to the bottom of a problem you are discussing with an employee. What blind spots do they have in finding a solution? What have they hidden which you need to know more about? Sometimes selected self-disclosure on your part may encourage them to be more open.

Praise

It is sometimes pointed out that 'appraisal' is based on the word 'praise'. Unfortunately that is the bit that is so often missed out in interviews. Yet knowing when and how to praise someone who is learning to do a new job or acquire a new skill pays off many times over. Different people need different amounts of praise and at different intervals. Praise must be seen to be earned, or it becomes debased. Try to link praise to the achievement of agreed objectives and milestones. This reinforces the message that planning a development project pays off; progress is being made.

Challenge

There are undoubtedly moments in helping people learn at work when you may need to challenge their ideas, attitudes or way of doing things. This has to be achieved assertively and not aggressively. You are probably familiar with the difference between assertiveness and aggression. Assertiveness is making clear your rights whilst respecting the rights of others. When you are assertive you are aiming for a 'win–win' outcome; that is, one where both parties gain something. This usually involves an element of compromise for both parties, to ensure that winning is not all on one side. Aggression is claiming your rights at the expense of other people's rights. The result is a 'win–lose' situation, the aggressor being the apparent winner, although aggressive managers may win the battle but usually lose the war.

People may choose to behave in a compliant way when faced with aggression. This would be characterized as a 'lose–win' encounter, where you concede your rights to pacify your aggressor.

The least productive engagement is where manipulation is used and neither party really asserts their rights; the result is a 'lose–lose' encounter.

In striving for a learning relationship with your staff you need to work towards 'win–win' outcomes where neither party has to deny or lose their most important rights and where it is possible to have an adult assertion of views and ideas without fear or favour.

Give and receive feedback

To give and receive feedback positively and effectively in a manager–employee relationship calls for distinct skills. Think of the different ways you react to critical views outside work. You can no doubt take quite firm comments from some of your friends, whereas the same views expressed by other friends or family might trigger a defensive reaction in you.

Here are some rules that you can test the next time you have the opportunity to give feedback or receive it. To be useful, feedback needs to be:

- objective and not judgemental;
- specific and illustrated by observed behaviour;
- relevant to the needs of the person being helped;
- relative to behaviour that the recipient has some chance of changing;
- given as soon after the event as possible.

Feedback is most effective when people ask for it, rather than when it is offered to them without their asking. Feedback is of course a waste of time if you engage in it in such a way that the employee resists hearing or using what you offer, or if they are not ready to hear or use it for a whole host of reasons. Some of these reasons will lie in the 'façade' pane of the Johari window which they are trying to hide from you. Some will be in the 'unknown' pane and will not be clear to you or the employee.

Help people to plan

In appraisal interviews there are opportunities for drawing up plans with an employee. At other intervals during the year you may have the opportunity to work together to plan development tasks and projects. These may be modest in scale but should combine the purposefulness of being part of a real job with the opportunity to learn new skills or knowledge. At each occasion you can provide practical examples of how to plan projects and find solutions to problems which will stand the member of staff in good stead in other work situations.

The following are the stages in planning which you might encourage a diffident learner to work through with you.

1   Define the situation which you want to change – for example, 'I lack confidence in using the office database and therefore fail to update customer records often enough.'

2   Define the objective(s) – for example, 'to learn how to create a new record and edit existing ones, to format a record to generate an address label'.

3   Identify obstacles to achieving the objective – for example, 'I feel put down by my supervisor, so I try to avoid showing I don't know how to do it. I have not been offered any time off to train.'

4   Identify possible solutions – for example:
    • 'Sack my supervisor!' or 'Come clean with my supervisor';
    • 'Ask for some coaching from a colleague who is very confident with the database';
    • 'Ask my manager for time and support to attend a course'.

Out of this process can come a firm commitment by the employee to attend a part-time course at the local college and to seek more help from colleagues and even the dreaded supervisor. You as their manager will want to complete the planning process by seeing why the supervisor is having this effect and maybe ask them to take responsibility for arranging the course.

Any good plan will include some decision on how the outcome is to be evaluated. In this case it might be achieving a certificate at the end of the course but, much more to the point, it should be competent performance of the tasks defined in the objectives, to the satisfaction of the supervisor. You may also, as the manager, discuss the outcome with both the employee and the supervisor. What have they both learnt from the exercise?

Know when not to intervene

Remember not to keep pulling up the seedling to see how the roots are growing. It is possible to take such an interest in the way someone is learning that they feel under test and very threatened. Agree a contract with your employee so you both know when and why it will be useful to meet to review progress.

The other key lesson to learn is to know when it is best to let someone proceed, secure in their new-found knowledge or skill. You do not want people to grow dependent on you; it is neither good for them nor for you. One important outcome of learning is that it enables you to do more by yourself; independence is liberating – dependence is a continuing drain on your time and energy.

Creating a learning environment

In a sense the rest of this book is about ways of creating a learning environment for your staff. This might mean literally setting up a learning centre where they come individually or in groups to learn either with a trainer or from self-study materials. There is more on this in Chapter 9, 'Using open learning'.

However, the way the term 'learning environment' is used here is more wide ranging than this. Some workplaces are run in such a way that the idea of learning on or off the job hardly features in anyone's thinking. How evident is it to your employees that you value their interest in learning? Would a visitor to your plant, office, studio or centre pick up any impression that you were striving to develop a learning organization? Let's consider some of the ways in which you can create an environment that is conducive to learning.

The way staff approach problems

When there is a problem, for example, a hold-up in production or a quality or customer care issue, how do staff tend
to react? Do they pass the buck or blame you and other
managers? If so, you have some uphill work to do on creating
an environment in which managers and staff work together
to meet customer needs more effectively.

Alternatively, staff may be encouraged to find and record
solutions to problems and share them with others. This may
be done through a suggestion box, or a reward system as a
way of saying thank you for saving the organization money
through reduced waste. Good ideas need to be harvested and
shared around. They may be written up as new operating
procedures or standards so that you move the performance
of your work group progressively up the quality slope. They
may also merit being reported in any departmental or organization-wide newsletter. Looking to the workforce as a main
resource for problem solving is a very powerful way of
showing that yours is an organization where learning matters.

The way staff approach appraisal

Whether or not you have a formal appraisal scheme, judgements about performance are always being made in the
workplace. How receptive are staff to giving and receiving
feedback? Does this sort of feedback tend to flow only down-
wards or are you and other managers open to receive
messages about your own approach to work and the way the
organization is operating?

If you have a formal appraisal scheme, has it become stuck
in the rut of bureaucracy? Is it regarded as a chore by all
concerned, and do interviews become more and more
overdue? If so, consider where decisions about the quality of
performance are really being made. Spend time re-examining
the weaknesses of your appraisal scheme and have the
courage to make fundamental changes. A malfunctioning
scheme is like a visible tombstone marking the demise of

all the good original intentions to encourage learning and development.

In Chapter 12, 'Assessing learning outcomes', you will find more help on using appraisal schemes to encourage greater openness and learning.

The way staff approach training and development

Do you have a comprehensive training and development programme? If so, how high on people's agendas is the programme? Are there some staff who have never been on a training event in all the years they have worked for the organization? Has the induction process fallen by the wayside or does it catch up with new staff only when they no longer need it? Are important changes introduced without any consideration being given to meeting the training needs that they generate?

Alternatively, there may be clear evidence on notice-boards, in personnel records and in the allocation of departmental training budgets that the need to invest in staff development is widely understood.

The way staff work with you

This chapter has featured the type of relationship that you may establish with your staff in order to promote a learning environment. Everyone has their own skills and experience to bring to this process. As you will have read in Chapter 1, 'How people learn at work', we all have our own preferred learning style. However, as a manager you are undoubtedly in a very strong position to set standards and values on learning as a natural and vital part of work. If it matters to you, it will begin to matter to your staff. As they see you model the approaches of the staff developer, so they in turn will begin to help others learn.

In the next chapter you can read about important areas of management to do with improving performance. It is easy in a book on training and development to forget that some problems need to be tackled by redesigning working procedures rather than by training interventions. Your task is to ensure that the staff you manage are given the chance to make their fullest individual contribution to the success of your organization. To enable them to do this you have to remove as many obstacles as possible and create a management system that people can work with.

Summary

First, you considered your role in helping people learn. This was described as a fundamental management process of analysing learning needs and working with the member of staff to ensure that such needs are met.

The main part of the chapter was concerned with the skills you need to help people learn. These range from demonstrating good learning behaviours yourself, through praising and challenging, to knowing when to intervene. The chapter concluded with some suggestions on creating a learning environment, including a review of the way staff approach problems, the way they approach appraisal and how they work with you.

Reading on

Downes, S. (1995), *Learning at Work*, London: Kogan Page. (This book offers effective strategies for making learning at work happen. Myths, pitfalls and blockages which inhibit learning are exposed, and practical remedies described and illustrated.)

Hayes, J. (1996), *Developing the Manager as Helper*, London: Routledge. (Presents a six-stage model for managers who want to help their employees develop. Chapter 8 is particularly useful on the application of the Johari window to offering feedback and challenging assumptions.)

■ 3

Improving performance

In this chapter you will be asked to identify those performance gaps which can be solved by changes in the way you manage your work and your people. In the next chapter we shall look at performance shortfalls which are caused because staff have not been properly trained for the job. For the moment, though, you are asked to think about whose responsibility it is to improve performance and to take a hard look at how you can ensure performance improvement in your staff.

The aim of this chapter is to help you to identify those aspects in your staff's performance which need to be improved by changes in the way you manage them and the environment in which they work. To achieve this you will be asked to:

- *identify some typical performance problems that managers face;*
- *analyse the common causes of such problems;*
- *plan steps to reduce them.*

These are the topics you will be reading more about:

- *who is responsible for performance improvement?*
- *why do things go wrong?*
- *identifying the causes and putting things right;*
- *what has this got to do with learning in the workplace?*

Who is responsible for performance improvement?

The short answer is you. One of your key roles is to manage the performance of individuals and groups. When things go wrong, you will want to know why and to take action to improve them. Spotting gaps in performance may sometimes be only too easy. Finding out how to improve performance requires skill, planning and maybe some honest self-appraisal on your part. It could be, for example, that you are inadvertently contributing to the problem by not creating an environment where performance can grow.

One of the paradoxes of being a manager is that whilst it is your final responsibility to ensure that standards are set and products and services delivered to those standards, you can only do this if your employees are competent, motivated and working to your overall leadership. In other words, your purpose as a manager can only be achieved through, and with, the willing co-operation of your staff.

Why do things go wrong?

An in-house trainer reports the following situation:

> A departmental manager approached me to discuss a problem of underperformance in his front-line staff. 'I can't afford any more gaffes at the reception desk. They're all as bad as each other. I've told them that I know customers can be a pain and always want the earth. I can remember when I was a junior putting up with all that flak. Can you lay on a course on communications and din it into them that they must not argue the toss with customers when things go wrong?'
>
> The trainer sensibly started by saying that a course might be provided at the right time, but that he thought there should be some work done beforehand to establish the nature and scale of the problem. The manager's first response was unhelpful: 'I'll manage them; you train them.'
>
> The trainer explained that training was not always effective as a first response to a problem and that if the manager wanted

value from the trainer's service, he had to decide whether to accept the contract the trainer was offering. This involved first having the chance of a longer discussion with the manager and some time with the staff to see what the job involved, how it was organized and what problems they were experiencing, individually and as a group.

What problems would you want to investigate further, if you were the trainer? Use any impressions and clues you have picked up about the manager and the work he is managing.

You probably reached the conclusion that it is the manager, in fact, who needs to take stock of his own approach to listening to, and talking with, employees or customers. His abrasive style has rubbed off on those he manages and, more importantly, the basic value of giving excellent customer care has got lost. The manager is obviously out of date and out of touch with the normal day-to-day experience of doing the job and hears about problems only when they become crises. His autocratic style of management has probably built up a divide between 'him' and 'us', the staff. He still thinks things can be 'dinned into' people.

You may also have questioned why things are going wrong. What is it in the service provided that causes so many complaints? These were exactly the areas that the trainer investigated with the manager and they agreed that there were a number of management goals to be set and achieved first before providing communication skills training for the staff.

This simple example confirms the point that managers need to examine their own performance, and the total environment in which the work of their department or organization is done, before clutching at training courses as a cure-all. Read through the following list of reasons for poor performance.

1 The staff could do the work but are not properly prepared for it.
2 They are square pegs in a round hole.
3 The work is beyond their capacity.

4   The work is too easy for them and they have lost all sense of challenge.
5   They are struggling to come to terms with organizational changes which they see as damaging to their interests.
6   They have experienced a serious setback at work and this has reduced their confidence.
7   They are involved in an interpersonal dispute or other people problems at work.
8   They have health problems or other difficulties outside work.
9   The job is ill-conceived.
10 The job is unnecessary.
11 They are inappropriately managed or supervised.
12 They have not been given the right equipment to do the job.
13 Their physical working environment is not conducive to good performance.
14 The sequence of their work is badly planned and wasteful in time and materials.
15 They do not feel sufficiently valued or rewarded, so they have given up trying.
16 They may be heavily dependent on the performance and delivery of others, who are letting them down.
17 They have too much to do.
18 They do not have enough to do.

We shall consider these reasons for poor performance more carefully later. The general message is to make sure that your management decisions and approaches do not reduce performance.

Identifying the causes and putting things right

To help think about under-performance in your workforce, it is useful to divide up the list of typical reasons given in the previous section. We can group them broadly in the following ways:

- a mismatch between the person and the job;
- reduced motivation and security as a result of change and/or interpersonal factors;
- management deficiencies, including inappropriate job design and resourcing, job satisfaction and reward, and work-load.

As you will see in a moment, this last set of reasons labelled 'management deficiencies' is the biggest, and this is the area over which you can have the most direct control. Whilst you can probably do little significantly to alter the environment of the whole organization or, beyond it, the market in which you operate, you can decide to do something about the way you manage your own staff.

You may also notice how many items in the list are behavioural and to do with the powerful effects of motivation and confidence. If you are seriously interested in improving performance, you have to accept that an important management task is to help people retain and increase motivation and encourage them to talk about how they feel about work assignments.

We can now take each of these topics in turn and consider why under-performance occurs and what you may be able to do about it.

A mismatch between the person and the job

Under this heading are grouped the first four reasons.

1 The staff could do the work but are not properly prepared for it.
2 They are square pegs in a round hole.
3 The work is beyond their capacity.
4 The work is too easy for them and they have lost all sense of challenge.

In each of these situations, either something has gone wrong at the stage of selection and recruitment or the job has changed around the person and they have not been able to adapt to the new work. We shall talk about reason 1 at the end of the chapter. The 'square peg' dilemma in reason 2 is familiar to most managers. Take care, though, that you do not attribute to nature what might be solved through the right kind of nurture. It is easy to be too hasty in making the judgement that someone will never change or improve in a particular job because they were 'born like that'. True, all jobs consist of a particular set of tasks, some of which come more naturally to some people than to others. A certain amount can be achieved through training and development and by reinforcing the motivation the employee feels when they are faced with tasks which they know they do not like doing.

Having taken all this into account, you will from time to time know that there is no point in continuing to press X to be more systematic and tidy when, despite all their best endeavours, they cannot manage it. The same would be true of the person who is in a job needing flair and imagination, who can only play safe and produce routine and uninspired work. If you suspect that you are trying to force a square peg into a round hole, you need to take the initiative by establishing what the profile of their performance really is. Start by talking to the person. Ask them what they feel they do best in their job.

Another approach to the problem is to measure what perceived demands a particular type of job makes. Think through the work and consider what mix of demands it makes. Does it, for example, call for someone who is a good finisher, or someone who can get a job going and have a lot of bright ideas about how best to do it? Some work calls for intense concentration for periods of time to ensure the accuracy of processes; other work depends on collecting, evaluating and acting on information. In other work interpersonal skills are essential, as much time is spent on the phone or talking with individuals or groups. If you have access to an assessment centre in your organization, you could ask the employee to complete a range of assessment activities, as much for their own benefit as yours. Such tests, based on a careful job analysis, will clarify for you the type of competences required for successful performance in this particular job.

Yet another area to explore is the shape of the hole into which the square peg was supposed to fit. Few jobs cannot be adapted or redesigned to get the best out of the jobholder. Few jobs are so isolated that the team cannot be adapted to compensate for weaknesses in individuals and exploit their particular talents. A well-balanced team needs a diversity of attributes and skills.

Reasons 3 – 'The work is beyond their capacity', and 4 – 'The work is too easy for them', describe problems which should be within your power to tackle. In the case of reason 3, if someone is clearly out of their depth in a particular role, your first step is to decide whether there is the will and the capacity to achieve the necessary knowledge and skills development to help them cope better.

If you think that the benefits of trying to do this are outweighed by the costs, you will need to decide on the future of this employee. Since it was not necessarily their fault that they found themselves in a job which was beyond them, you may feel that you have an obligation to find some better use for their contribution. Such a transition needs to be tackled very sensitively as the post-holder may well feel a loss of face and confidence. If, in the other hand, you approach the situation assertively and positively, they may in time thank you for relieving them of a job which had become a burden.

You should also seriously consider how the situation has arisen. It may be that you have inherited the consequence of a misjudged appointment made by your predecessor. You yourself may have made the appointment and you now need to think what you should do differently and better when you are making further appointments. Far too much reliance is placed on interviewing in staff selection. Interviews need to be very well conducted if they are to deliver objective results, and interviewing is a limited tool if you want to measure aspects of performance. If you have made costly mistakes in past appointments, consider using expert help to design a better selection process. This might be set up as an assessment centre and should include the use of psychometric testing and some simulation activities to see how applicants perform the tasks that are crucial to the job.

If, as in reason 4, you know that someone is coasting along

in a job which is way below their abilities, provided the work is up to standard you could take the attitude that that is their choice. On the other hand, you are unlikely to get quality, initiative or fresh thinking from a person who is totally unstretched by their job. They may feel trapped in their current position and think that you are not interested in what they could really do for the company. If they have deliberately chosen a soft option, they will soon become a source of irritation to others who are committed to growth and development.

The solution may be to use an appraisal interview to talk through with the person their current level of performance. Praise what is good. Explain that you need people who are prepared to take an active role in helping the organization to become more competitive and grow. Nothing stands still and organizations which are not striving for change and improvement risk going to the wall. Discuss what blockages they feel prevent them from doing more. Ask them what they would like to bring to the job. They may be relieved that at last they are being taken seriously. Agree three or four objectives which give them something to strive for. Make the objectives SMART. If you have not come across it before, the SMART acronym is very useful: S = Specific, M = Measurable, A = Achievable, R = Realistic, T = Time-bound. A SMART objective might read like this:

'You have agreed to produce proposals during the next month for reorganizing the system for receiving, logging and responding to customer complaints. You will circulate them to the section for discussion and comment and produce a short management report recommending the best options for implementation.'

In this example you can see that the objective is Specific and Measurable. As a manager you will also know whether or not it is Achievable and Realistic within the capacity of the individual. There is no point in setting up an objective which is unattainable. The objective in the example is also Time-bound; it has to be achieved within the next month.

In summary, it is wasteful to have people in the wrong slot. It does them no good and it certainly does not enhance the performance of the organization or department that you are managing.

Reduced motivation and security as a result of change and/or interpersonal factors

Under this heading is the next group of reasons for poor performance.

5   The staff are struggling to come to terms with organizational changes which they perceive to be damaging to their interests.
6   They have experienced a serious setback at work and this has reduced their confidence.
7   They are involved in an interpersonal dispute or other people problems at work.
8   They have health problems or other difficulties outside work.

People have different capacities to handle the uncertainty of change (reason 5). Consider the reaction to an announcement like this:

'The company has decided reluctantly that this plant will close, but there will be the possibility for most staff to transfer to our plant in the Midlands. Relocation packages will be offered to successful candidates. It is hoped to avoid compulsory redundancy, although this ...'

This level of change will induce a degree of organizational trauma which will make the management role very difficult for a while. Even when the unpalatable relocation programme has been completed, there will be tremors and aftershocks for some staff.

Consider how you yourself react when some decision is made which will affect your job. Less dramatic change may still have an effect on staff performance. If badly handled, a decision to redesign the layout of a work-space can cause confusion and drain energy and concentration from the key purposes of the staff involved. So in times of change – and that means all the time for most of us – expect that some people's performance may temporarily suffer. The experience of change has been compared to bereavement. At first you pretend it has not happened, whether it is a personal loss or the loss of a familiar work group, environment or task. Then you may become angry about it and resist it. Gradually, with the passage of time, it begins to make better sense to go along with the new order.

You can no sooner tell someone to snap out of grieving than you can tell an employee to like a new way of doing things. Both processes take their own time and if you can afford to live with this you will have kept their respect and be able to capitalize on their new commitment and energy when they have completed the change in their own minds.

Reason 6 – 'They have experienced a serious setback at work and this has reduced their confidence' – can be a very difficult one for a manager to work with. The best strategy is to try to make sure that the employee has some success with which to begin to wipe out the negative and energy-sapping influence of failure. If you missed the vital penalty which would have got your team into the semi-finals, it is going to take a success on a similar scale to make you feel really on top again. It does not have to be that you score the winning penalty in the next competition, although that would certainly lay the ghost of failure for many people. Use the learning that can be derived from mistakes and failure to plan positive change. As a manager you should devote time to reviewing failures and coaching staff to avoid them in the future.

Work squabbles and vendettas are seriously disruptive (reason 7); so, too, are liaisons and friendships which get in the way of quality work performance.

A manager reports:

I knew I was going to have to intervene when Jill spoke to me. She is the only woman in my team of manual staff and Brian has really got it in for her; he cannot stand working with her. This morning it has come to a head and I now wish I had had the courage to act sooner.

Jill called me down to the depot. I had already separated them by putting them on different shifts. When I arrived, Jill showed me the chaos on the depot floor. All her gear had been thrown out of the van in a heap. The tank had been drained of diesel. She was very upset and accused Brian of doing it. It seems likely because he has to hand over the van to her at the end of his shift. She then told me that the last time they were on the same shift he drove his van, with the headlights blazing, right behind hers all round the estate and forced her to stop and leave her vehicle.

If this is true, and I fear it is, I should have started a disciplinary with Brian already; I need to talk to him urgently, before this gets completely out of hand. He has to know that his job is on the line.

This real-life story is a sad reminder both of what can happen when squabbles and bad feeling are allowed to fester in the workplace and also what a trap you can lay for yourself as a manager if you do not take action in good time.

Finally, you may be dealing with poor performance because of health problems or other difficulties outside work (reason 8). More and more organizations are setting up employee assistance programmes (EAPs) which can provide confidential help and counselling. Your organization may also have its own in-house occupational health service. Your role is to spend enough time with your staff to be able to notice reductions in performance which may be caused by these problems. You are not required to investigate people's personal lives, nor are most managers qualified to do so. Focus on the work performance and, if you have a good enough relationship with your staff, they may choose to be open with you about other problems which are getting in the way. If you work in a small organization, you are even more likely to be aware of what is going on in people's lives. This can be good or bad, depending on the quality of group relations. Organizations of whatever size need to keep a balance between focusing on what needs to be done to achieve the task and meeting the needs of the group and the individuals in it. We can all probably remember work groups which forgot about the task they were set up to achieve because they were having such a good time being a group.

In a small organization you will not have in-house medical

or counselling resources, so you will need to have a list of external providers of help. You cannot, of course, require someone to seek counselling. All you can do is to provide them with information and friendly support. Should they decide to seek help, arrange for them to have some time off to attend appointments.

Management deficiencies

As this chapter has so far shown, the manager must be active in finding solutions to problems of poor performance, some of which may well be of his or her own making.

In this last section consider briefly the following range of reasons which are undoubtedly down to you.

This set includes the rest of the list we started with, but it can be further subdivided into:

- inappropriate job design and resourcing;
- low job satisfaction and inadequate reward;
- inappropriate work-load.

Inappropriate job design and resourcing

Under this sub-heading are included the following reasons.

9   The job is ill-conceived.
10   The job is unnecessary.
11   Employees are inappropriately managed or supervised.
12   They have not been given the right equipment to do the job.
13   Their physical working environment is not conducive to good performance.
14   The sequence of their work is badly planned and wasteful in time and materials.

Even if a job is not ill-conceived, it may need to be thoroughly rethought as the environment of the business changes around it. So, when a vacancy occurs, use the opportunity to consider whether you need another person occupying this role and doing this particular range of tasks. You may discover that it is unnecessary and can be combined with other roles. Of course you should not wait for the clear field of a vacancy before you address situations referred to in reasons 9 or 10. You need to go back to your business plan and see how the inappropriate jobs may be redefined, and to do so in discussion with the post-holders. Also ask yourself how the situation arose in the first place. Staffing is almost certainly your biggest overhead, so you cannot afford to squander it.

Inappropriate management or supervision (reason 11) will quickly de-motivate and lead to loss of performance. If you honestly feel that you are part of the problem, plan a management development programme for yourself and discuss it with your manager. If you do not feel you know enough to do this, consider finding a mentor or external consultant to guide you. You may also consider approaching your local university or college, your Business Link or Training and Enterprise Council (TEC), for guidance on management development opportunities in your area. If you do not like the idea of attending courses away from home, try the Open University Business School or distance learning programmes for managers which other universities provide.

If bad workers blame their tools, it is equally true that good workers are wasted unless they have the equipment to do the job. The same is true of poor physical environment. Stress levels will mount if rooms are not adequately heated or ventilated, or are over-crowded. Reason 14 – 'Bad operational sequences', is a question of job design, and in more enlightened work settings committed to total quality, all staff will be thinking about ways to improve constantly the organization of the work to reduce wastage.

Low job satisfaction and inadequate reward

15 Staff do not feel sufficiently valued or rewarded, so they have given up trying.
16 They may be heavily dependent on the performance and delivery of others, who are letting them down.

Of all the things that you as a manager can do to boost performance, valuing achievement in your employees' work is probably the most powerful. If you rarely thank them for work well done, they will think it is not worth making that extra effort. The question of reward is part of the same picture, although most managers do not have great latitude in varying financial reward except through profit sharing or through commission. In a number of research projects performance-related pay has been shown to be less effective as a motivator than its advocates would claim. The level of financial reward which such schemes deliver is not usually high enough to make any real difference to motivation.

If you are concerned about putting the thank you message over to staff who give more than expected, you may be able to identify other types of reward, such as involving them in key decisions, offering them staff development opportunities, arranging exchange or study visits with other organizations in the UK or abroad. For some staff what they will most appreciate is to be given extra responsibility and the prospect of promotion.

Reason 16 – 'Dependence on others, who are letting them down' – provides a reminder that in judging any performance you have to take into account not just the individual but also the team. It will be very de-motivating for staff if you draw attention to poor performance without identifying the source of the poor quality or bottle-necks which may lie up-stream of their work. Managers have to be regularly in touch with all aspects of the work they are responsible for and it is up to you to spot the difficulties, and to work to solve them, with the staff who are experiencing them.

Inappropriate work-load

17   Staff have too much to do.
18   They do not have enough to do.

This final pair of reasons is equally worthy of your attention. Monitoring work-load can prevent the build-up of stress and poor performance. It is stressful to be at a loose end; we all need some stimulus, and boredom at work is very corrosive.

If you let things go to the other extreme and allow or require people to work too long hours or under unremitting pressure without any clear source of support, you run the risk of losing quality of production or services. You may also contribute to occupational stress in your employees which leads to sick-leave and in some cases may cause breakdown or coronary disease. There is an increasing number of court cases being brought against employers whose negligence in these areas may render them liable to the settlement of substantial claims.

What has this to do with learning in the workplace?

We learn through mistakes, and as a manager part of your learning is to identify reasons why people under-perform and to take appropriate steps to help them do better. What you learn in the process increases your repertoire of management skills. Even when an intervention does not achieve the immediate results you hoped for, you are still learning about how to deal with that individual or learning how to adapt your approach so that you manage better next time.

You are also helping the people you manage to learn that poor performance is not the norm and that it is possible to improve a badly designed job or to reduce an excessive work-load. Once people feel more in control of their circumstances at work, their stress levels will drop and they will feel more able to perform to standard. This is a profoundly important piece of learning which will condition all their work experience with you.

Finally, you will remember reason 1 – 'The staff could do the work but are not properly prepared for it'. There are of course situations where the only way to improve performance is to provide some form of training and development. In the next chapter you will find out how to assess learning needs, and in the following chapters you can plan how to meet them.

Summary

The responsibility for improving performance is yours although, paradoxically, you can only achieve this with the willing co-operation of your staff.

You considered a range of 18 reasons why things go wrong. These reasons were then sorted into the following sets:

- a mismatch between the person and the job;
- reduced motivation because of change and/or interpersonal factors;
- management deficiencies;
- inappropriate job design and resourcing;
- low job satisfaction and inadequate reward;
- inappropriate work-load.

In each case you were given some guidance on measures to improve performance. Finally, the connection was made between improving performance and encouraging learning in the workplace.

Reading on

Bentley, T. (1997) *Bridging the Performance Gap*, Aldershot: Gower. (This book will help you identify the gap between an individual's performance and their potential.)

■ 4

Learning needs and how to analyse them

How do you know when there are learning needs to be met in your work group? It may be that someone's performance falls below requirements. It may be that you can see that someone has the potential to make a bigger contribution but they need help to develop the necessary skills, knowledge and confidence. You may have introduced some new computer software or set up a new system of working, which will mean that your staff need to be properly prepared to use it. Every time a new member of staff joins your work group they bring with them learning needs. These may include technical training needs as well as the need to be introduced to your organization.

If you adopt the line argued through this book, all learning needs at work can be met by various training and development activities. These may range from attending a day-release course to working with a mentor while you tackle a new assignment. So, in an ideal world, you will be identifying and analysing learning needs on a continuing basis as part of the learning relationship effective managers strive to establish with their staff. It might be that you have a concern about individual or group performance; or you may anticipate a need that is about to occur and plan how to meet it before a performance problem begins to build up.

The aim of this chapter is to help you to develop a systematic way of finding out what learning needs your workforce has and plan how to meet them. To achieve this you will be asked to:

- *base your identification of learning needs on evidence gathered in the workplace;*
- *analyse needs to find practical solutions.*

These are the topics you will be reading more about:

- *learning needs – how to identify and analyse them;*
- *analysing individual learning needs;*
- *analysing group learning needs.*

Learning needs – how to identify and analyse them

In many organizations there is an annual training needs analysis. This provides the information on which the corporate training plan is based. Analysing information for the whole organization would normally be the responsibility of internal or external trainers. In this chapter we are going to look at how you can use these basic principles to identify the learning needs of individuals and groups you manage. Often the process will be quite informal and will involve the people who have the learning needs. Always check any hunches you have about performance gaps by talking them over with the staff concerned. It could be that they see things differently and simply want you to understand that you should organize the work differently. As you know from reading the previous chapter, some performance problems may be of your own making or an outcome of the way the organization is or is not responding to change. Training is not always the answer. Even if it is, it is better to talk over the need with the person concerned and discuss different ways of solving it through training. In this way they are much more likely to approach whatever activity is selected with some enthusiasm and motivation.

What is a learning need?

The simplest definition of a learning need is 'a gap between current performance and required performance, which can best be met by training and development'. So we can straight away scotch the idea that you identify learning needs by checking to see what courses someone has or has not been on; identifying learning needs is concerned with the lack of skills, knowledge and experience which is preventing satisfactory performance in the job. By basing the process of needs identification on performance and not on course participation or exam results, you can make a better analysis of what to do about meeting the need.

How do you identify learning needs?

To identify learning needs you have to examine two things: the job and the jobholder. You will need to understand:

- the requirements of the job and the standards of performance expected of someone doing the job well;
- what the person can currently do, or what might be called their profile of performance in the job.

Know the job

First, think about the requirements of the job. This means doing a job analysis. You may feel that you know the job inside out; you may have even done it yourself. However, it may still be useful to remind yourself about the way the job has been described in writing. Try the job description as a general broadbrush statement and look for more detail in working procedures and objectives that have been agreed in appraisal interviews with your employee.

For example, if, among other things, the job description requires the post-holder to keep financial records of income and expenditure for a section, you will expect them to have bookkeeping expertise and to know how to operate your financial software to provide up-to-date and accurate records. The person specification which accompanies the job description will probably use such words as 'systematic, orderly and numerate'.

What do you do if the job description is sketchy or out of date, and does not yield the sort of information you need? The first answer is to improve the job description, and to involve the post-holder in this. You will justifiably run into personnel problems if you alter or load a job description without discussing it with the post-holder. (You might also ask how the situation of sloppy or inadequate job descriptions arose in the first place. Perhaps you inherited the problem; consult your personnel specialist, if you have one, or seek the advice of an experienced human resource management consultant.)

If you do not have a ready-made start in the documents which describe the job, go back to the question, 'What is the main purpose of this job?'. It might be, for example, 'to manage the sales office to ensure that orders are processed accurately on the day of receipt'. Then concentrate on what the jobholder needs to do to achieve this purpose. This will usually break down into four or five principal tasks, which in this case might be:

1 monitoring work-flow and ensuring adequate staff resources to meet demand;
2 processing orders and sales data for the rest of the organization;
3 managing sales office staff;
4 maximizing customer satisfaction by keeping them fully informed;
5 preparing departmental plans and budgets.

Within each of these you can then identify a number of performance objectives. For example, within the task 'Managing sales office staff' there might be an objective to 'Conduct performance appraisals with each member of staff using the company's appraisal scheme'.

Make these objectives as precise and measurable as possible. Link them to any existing standards that operate in your organization. For example, by referring to the company's appraisal scheme in your objective it is not then necessary to spell out that there should be an annual formal appraisal and informal quarterly appraisals, or that employees should be encouraged to give feedback to their managers. This will be contained in the company procedures for appraisal.

Avoid using woolly words. Having as clear as possible an idea of the requirements of the job and the competences that jobholders will need to demonstrate in order to perform it well provides a firm foundation not only for training needs analysis but also for most of the other important management functions, such as selection, promotion, appraisal, disciplinaries and dismissal.

It is worth remembering that the requirements of any job do not remain static. Technologies, for example, are constantly evolving. Supposing a new update of a computer package is bought for your office which includes a dozen or so improved methods of working that make new processes possible or take the chore out of existing ones. Unless people realize these features create opportunities for greater efficiency, they will stick to what they know and the actual and the opportunity costs of the new update will be wasted.

There are, however, many other reasons why jobs do not stay the same. You could say that any job you manage should be changing and improving in some way. For example, managers taking part in appraisal training sometimes say that they cannot think of new objectives for some of the jobs they appraise.

'I just want the typists to carry on typing accurately and fast', said a manager of a clerical services pool in a government department. In discussion, however, they had to admit that there were things which could be done differently and better. Most of all they recognized that by setting the same objectives year after year they were imprisoning the employees. Of course, the basic task of typing needed to be done to a required standard, although what this might be was not always discussed and quantified. But what else could employees do to improve the efficiency and performance of the department? How ready were they to assume greater responsibility for quality issues, for developing better work systems and achieving a higher level of customer satisfaction?

To do this some of them would need further training and development of one sort or another. This might be no more complicated than providing an opportunity to work in a structured way on a small development project to reorganize work allocation and progress logging. The manager could decide, with the member of staff, on objectives for the project, any coaching they might need and what outcomes might be expected. This would be a development task for which the employee would be allowed some time free from the basic word processing duties that formed the core of the job.

Know the person

The second aspect of identifying learning needs is knowing the profile of performance of the employee. You may have thought as you read the example in the previous paragraph that some of your staff would jump at the chance of being asked to do a special project and others would bury their heads in their work and hope the threat of more challenging work would go away.

To make effective decisions about learning needs you do need to know what level of competence people have already attained and to be able to make some sensible judgements about their readiness to learn through further training and development. If you conduct regular performance appraisals with your staff, using an agreed set of standards and objectives, you should have a clear idea about their levels of competence. If you do not currently have a performance appraisal scheme in your organization, what you are learning in this chapter about needs analysis will be very useful if you decide to set one up. Planning how to meet learning needs is one important consequence of staff appraisal.

Readiness to learn is harder to measure unless you have the opportunity to talk through training needs and sound out the attitudes and commitment of the individual concerned. The same is true of measuring potential to learn. There are psychological tests which can give indications of people's potential in different functions and roles. These, however, have to be administered by a suitably qualified person, often within a development centre. In practice, you may adopt a rule of thumb of getting to know your staff through working with them and always expecting the most from them. People perform to such expectations. If you as a manager expect very little, very little is what you will normally get.

Analysing needs to find solutions

Identification is one-half of the process of learning needs analysis. There is no point, however, in discovering that employees have a need unless you can work out what to do about it. It may well be that the solution has become evident in the process of identifying the need. For example, the answer to lack of technical expertise in operating a piece of equipment is likely to be providing training. (You may of course have reached the conclusion that the individual showed so little aptitude that they would be better employed on some other range of tasks which they could handle more confidently; but this would indicate that you or a predecessor had made a bad appointment in the first place.) If training is the answer, you then have to choose from a range of solutions. These are more fully described in the next seven chapters of this book. You may decide to:

- find the best available training opportunity and prepare the employee to get the most out of the chosen course (Chapters 5, 'Choosing training events' and 6, 'Getting the best out of training events');
- find a more experienced operator in your group who can coach the employee (Chapter 7, 'Developing your staff as they work');
- arrange for them to work at another plant where they can have more practical experience and tuition (Chapter 8, 'Training and development opportunities outside the workplace');
- find an open learning package which teaches the process and skills required, so that the employee can learn in the plant, in a learning centre or at home, using a more experienced colleague as a coach (Chapter 9, 'Using open learning');
- plan and run your own training event which is very much geared to the needs of your work group (Chapter 10, 'Planning a training event' and Chapter 11, 'Delivering a training event').

In practice there will be a number of factors which affect your choice. These may include:

- organizational factors such as your training and development policy and funding;
- management factors – you may find it difficult to allow the members of staff to be away at a particular time because of work pressure;
- individual factors – people have their own learning styles and preferences;
- training factors – you can choose only from what is available and you will need to balance quality against cost and accessibility.

Analysing individual learning needs

Here are some examples of learning needs in the workplace; how many do you see in your own work group?

The learning needs of poor performers

Supposing there is someone in your work group who has made a mistake which has taken time and effort to put right. The person just cannot see how to perform better at present and maybe they are as worried about it as you, even if they are trying hard not to show it. Or, worse still, they may have lost motivation to do any better.

You realize that they need to learn to meet the requirements of the job. You assume that it is partly a question of their improving their skills in handling this type of work. They may also need to be better informed; they may lack some essential knowledge and this may be what is causing the mistakes.

Your management task in such situations is to analyse what is needed – is it skills practice, or an input of information, or both? Then you can help an employee learn to improve poor performance, provided you can overcome either their lack of awareness of a learning need or, possibly, their resistance to exposing this performance weakness.

Learning to improve good performance

Consider the following situation. You realize that someone you manage wants to expand their horizons. They are performing confidently and competently and are looking out for new opportunities. Saying to someone in this situation 'Would you like to learn how to operate this or take on this new responsibility?' will be received positively. They will know that they are ready for a new challenge, particularly if it brings with it the prospect of greater recognition and respect. If you do not recognize when people are showing this type of learning readiness you will eventually kill off their wish to learn and either they will start to think about moving on or, worse still, they may lose their commitment and become disaffected. If your organization is operating in a way that stifles initiative and readiness to learn, you too will be a victim at some point. Learning is about flexibility in meeting needs and finding new solutions. No organization can thrive if it suppresses the urge to learn.

Your management task with the competent and willing employee is to support their enthusiasm to learn and judge how much challenge to offer them so that they move forward with confidence to a new performance level.

In both cases, learning involves not just the mind and the hands but also the feelings and the sense of identity and worth of the employee. Nothing can happen until and unless there is motivation.

Analysing group learning needs

Important changes in your organization's mission, structure, rate of growth, technology and location all prompt you to think again about analysing learning needs. Even if this year things are more stable than last and there are no major upheavals on the horizon, you may still be aware, from your knowledge of the business, that there are some general problems which need to be addressed during a period of comparative quiet. It may be that in working with individuals to identify learning needs, common strands crop up.

For example:

> In organization X there has been evidence of people not being
> prepared to take the initiative or say what they really feel about
> work. This has been accompanied by a lot of buck passing and
> blaming of others, particularly those who manage them. This
> leads the manager to the conclusion that it would be valuable
> to try to break through this deadlock and achieve a more open
> organization where it is possible to learn from mistakes and
> draw on the energy and ideas of the whole workforce. This is
> all the more urgent because the market in which they operate
> is highly competitive and some of the main rival concerns have
> been sounding off recently about becoming learning organiza-
> tions and committing themselves to becoming world-class
> manufacturers.

If you were the manager, how would you use what you
know about learning needs analysis to clarify your thoughts
and plan to act? You will need to be quite specific about the
group learning need. It may perhaps be focused on communications and relationships.

You might consider enlisting a group of employees to help
you quantify the problem. You might also ask an external
consultant to work with you so that the objectivity and facilitation of the project is ensured. Questions which might be
asked during the identification of learning needs might
include the following.

- Where are the communications blockages?
- Why do people think they happen?
- What are the most effective channels of communication?
  What are the least?
- What do people most want to inform others about and
  hear about? What least?
- Does some information get screened out from some
  people and, if so, why?
- What can we try to improve the way we communicate?
- What can we scrap tomorrow, and it would make no
  difference?

- What can we introduce tomorrow, and it would make a world of difference?
- Is it safe to say you have made a mistake and, if not, why?
- What can be done to achieve a 'no-blame' culture?
- How can improved communications make us more productive and competitive?

You might agree that the trainer should conduct a series of individual interviews across the whole organization and hold some focus groups where people can work on answers to some of the questions in an open and constructive way. You might also decide to visit some other companies to try to benchmark yourself against good practice. It would be naïve to expect your rivals to let you in, but you can learn a lot from other companies who are of similar standing but not in competition with you. How have they improved communications and gained greater commitment?

All this information can be drawn together and analysed. If you are too busy to do this yourself, pay your trusted consultant to do it for you. You should be able to identify where the priority training needs are. It may be, for example, that your senior management team has not fully clarified the direction and the targets for the company. They are therefore not giving a lead by creating and sharing a vision, and as a consequence the organization is turning in on itself in uncertainty and self-doubt. Middle management may feel itself trapped between directives from on high and pressure from below. Employees may have slipped back into the comfortable pose of blaming all the ills in the world on those above them. They may think that their views do not count and that if you stick your head up over the parapet you get shot.

Having identified these needs, how would you work out some solutions? You might decide to set up task groups to tackle key communications problems. These will need some external facilitation. Their membership can be drawn from all tiers of the organization and they need to have clearly defined terms of reference and levels of decision making. You might also commission an audit of your written communications to see how clearly and consistently you convey information. You could also aim to reduce paper messages by a significant factor. Training can be provided for first-line managers in how to run team-briefing sessions and senior management might be asked to take responsibility for ensuring that there is continuing momentum in change initiatives. They may also be asked to set up their own mentoring system, perhaps using colleagues from benchmark companies as mentors.

Inevitably, in thinking globally about changing cultures and developing the organization, solutions will need to be found in many different forms and over a period of time. Attempts which are too hasty and which are not properly embedded in the imagination of the workforce become branded as 'today's fashion'.

Summary

To identify learning needs, you have to be very clear about the requirements of the job and the level of competence of the jobholder. Once needs have been identified, you will then be looking for solutions. You were given a preview of Chapters 5–11 which offer guidance on both formal training and day-to-day development opportunities for your staff.

You concluded by thinking about the analysis of individual and group learning needs.

Remember that the process of learning needs analysis should not be too complicated, or it will simply not happen. Try to develop the habit of gathering information about training needs on a day-to-day basis as you work with your staff, and of thinking about ways of solving learning needs.

Having now considered how to analyse individual and group learning needs, you will be reading in the next six chapters about the range of solutions that you can draw on.

Reading on

Bartram, S. and Gibson, B. (1997), *Training Needs Analysis*, 2nd edn, Aldershot: Gower. (Provides 22 instruments and documents for gathering and analysing information about training and development issues in your organization.)

■ 5

Choosing training events

If you mention a training and development need to most people they think of going on a workshop or course. There are sometimes other ways of achieving the same or better results, so do not always start by looking for a course. Alternative approaches are available to you in your day-to-day work as a manager, and you can plan how to use these when you read Chapters 7–9.

For now, though, the focus is on identifying the place of training courses and workshops in your staff development plans; how, as a manager, can you ensure that they do contribute to people's learning?

Unfortunately, training does not always result in the learning experiences that you know your member of staff needs. So it is important to make choices thoughtfully. Your staff will respect you for it and they will realize that you place great value on the training you choose for them. In the next chapter you can consider how to get the best out of events once you have chosen them.

The aim of this chapter is to equip you to choose training events so that your staff learn in a purposeful way. To achieve this you will be asked to:

- *reflect on your own experience of attending courses;*
- *develop your capacity to choose events which offer to meet the learning needs of your staff;*
- *plan how you will use the next occasion when you send a member of staff on a training event, as an opportunity to improve your selection skills.*

You will also acquire some background information on finding courses and on accreditation and S/NVQs.

These are the topics you will be reading more about:

- *what is your experience of attending training events?*
- *what is your experience of choosing training events for your staff?*
- *choosing a training event;*
- *accreditation and S/NVQs;*
- *how, as a manager, can you reduce the risk of choosing the wrong course?*
- *in-house or external providers?*
- *choosing and using a trainer.*

What is your experience of attending training events?

You will have your own views on the value of courses and workshops and you can draw on this experience when planning how to use them to develop your own staff.

Reflect on the best course you have attended. What made it such a success? Note down several reasons.

You may have commented on the fact that you went with an initial enthusiasm to learn about the topic, or that you were quickly won over to it by the exciting way the trainer helped you learn. As I have said before, motivation is crucial. Occasionally, the need to know something is so intense that you can motivate yourself to learn even though the quality of the tuition is not high. Provided it unlocks the door and you find out how to discover more for yourself, that may be sufficient. So it is not just a question of how well the trainer performs, although good performance helps; it is also a question of what you bring to the event.

There are many other factors which you may have picked out. The pace, variety, level, stimulus and duration of the event will have affected not only how you felt about learning in this way but also how much you actually learnt.

The real test of a training event is the extent to which it helped you perform better, as a learner, as a worker, as a person.

What is your experience of choosing training events for your staff?

If you have already arranged for members of your staff to attend training events, check how well you are choosing from what is on offer. Make a brief note of one or two examples of good choices you have made. Then note for each some reasons why, such as, 'The events suited the needs of the person I sent', 'The reputation of the course provider was well known to me'.

If you have been unfortunate and chose a course which did not work for your member of staff, the next section should help you reduce the risk of it happening again.

Choosing a training event

Here is a checklist to take you through the main steps in selecting a training event.

1 Match the learning needs of the participant to the aims and objectives of the course or workshop – have you chosen the right event for your particular learner?
2 Distinguish between courses which contribute towards, or lead to a qualification, and those that do not – have you considered this, and have you found out what the learner would prefer? Longer courses can contribute towards an award and this benefit to the learner has to be weighed up against the cost in time and effort on their part and the fee costs and cover for absence that the organization has to meet.
3 Seek evidence of the quality of the training provision – if you have queries or concerns as a result of reading the brochure, have you spoken to the providers to resolve them?
4 Assess the terms and conditions – what does the brochure tell you about any means of redress you may have if you are not satisfied?
5 Pick the right point in time for the training – for example, is the training still appropriate or has the need passed?

6   Check the logistics – will the effort of getting to the training be too great? Will there need to be some child care support?

7   Choose between an open event run outside your organization and one run in-house – will the mix and experience of the other participants enhance or detract from the experience for your member of staff?

The main types of training event on offer

Courses

Courses tend to be taught by a lecturer, tutor or trainer; they are usually designed to impart knowledge or develop technical skills and resemble the process that we have all experienced at school or college. Vocational courses are a particular form of adult education and those which work well avoid the worst faults of some traditional college lecturing – that is, the lecturer recognizes that adults need to see the vocational relevance of what they are learning. Good courses also benefit from thorough planning and preparation, with good presentation methods.

Courses may be short, lasting for one to five days, or long, running over a period of months or years on a part-time basis as, for example, an MBA or a course leading to a professional qualification. The longer the course, the more likely it is to be provided by an academic institution and lead to a qualification.

Seminars

Seminars in an academic setting usually involve participants in preparing and making an oral presentation to which other students respond under the guidance of the tutor. In training, and in particular in management development, the word is often used to describe a presentation by an expert on a new process or topic, followed by some questions and answers.

Workshops

Workshops are designed to provide a learning environment in which people can reflect on their experience and practise skills and techniques. The workshop design tends to draw on the experience of the participants as an important resource. Workshops use a variety of participative techniques such as group discussions, simulation exercises, role-play and brainstorming. The tutor who runs them will adopt facilitative methods and will not offer to provide ready-made solutions to all the questions and issues that the group may raise. The responsibility for this is frequently handed back to the group or the individual, while the tutor offers support.

There are a few more exotic titles such 'symposium' – a gathering of experts who contribute papers on a particular topic, or the 'master class' – a fancy name for a workshop but one which may justifiably alienate a significant number of women participants. Conferences also provide learning opportunities. They are useful for current awareness and can be inspirational. You also have the advantage of meeting and discussing topics with other attendees.

You may also be able to choose between in-house or external training events. There is some guidance on this later in this chapter.

How do you find out what's available?

Start on your own doorstep. If you work in a medium-to-large organization with an in-house training unit, see what they have to offer. (There are some advantages and disadvantages to using in-house training, considered below.) Even if they cannot provide the training which your staff need, they will probably have their own database of other providers.

You can also approach:

- your local college or university;
- your nearest Business Link or Training and Enterprise Council (TEC) or Local Enterprise Council in Scotland (LEC);
- your chamber of commerce.

TAP databases, which are usually maintained by your nearest Business Link or TEC, contain listings of many local training courses and services.

For management development courses and workshops try directories such as:

The Management Training Directory
AP Information Services
Roman House
296 Golders Green Road
London NW1 9PZ
Telephone: 0181 455 4550

You might also approach the following organizations:

The Institute of Management
Management House
Cottingham Road
Corby
Northants NN17 1TT
Telephone: 01536 204222

Institute of Personnel and Development
35 Camp Road
Wimbledon
London
SW19 4UX
Telephone: 0181 971 9000

Association for Management Education and Development (AMED)
14–15 Belgrave Square
London
SW1X 8PS
Telephone: 0171 235 3505

If you are seeking training specific to your own specialism or profession, consult your professional body or see who is advertising in your professional journals.

Personal recommendation is another avenue to explore. Ask other managers doing similar work to yours. Ask whom they have used, and why they felt the event had been a success.

Accreditation and S/NVQs

Accreditation for prior learning and experience means giving people credit for what they can demonstrate they can already do. Some larger organizations issue their own certificates in recognition of achievements. Others have approached local universities or open college networks to have their training programmes accredited. It may be that a university will be prepared to validate part of a company training programme and offer one or more credits towards degree or diploma courses. The choices are opening up, and if you are planning a sustained programme of training and development in your organization it is worth considering the option of discussion your ideas with a local university.

You will also no doubt have heard about National Vocational Qualifications (abbreviated to NVQs, or more properly S/NVQs – the 'SVQ' denotes the Scottish form of the qualification). The S/NVQ is now regarded by many as the building block of vocational training and development. Most industry sectors have established standards of performance which can be assessed in the workplace. Successful assessment enables employees to accumulate S/NVQs which may lead to a qualification. The value of the NVQ for the employee is that it is a national and transferable recognition of competence at a particular level of performance. The organization can also show that its workforce is conforming to a national standard. Unlike awards based solely on exams, S/NVQs demonstrate competence on the job. Some employees will require training to bring them up to the necessary standard of competence for the functions they perform in their job. In competence-based training, explicit outcome-based standards are always used as the basis for preparing a training programme.

An employee prepares with the help of a manager or trainer, by first measuring their performance against the relevant standards and then deciding where they need additional training or work experience to prepare for assessment. Assessment is performed by qualified assessors and involves direct observation, wherever possible, and the reading of the candidate's portfolio of related material gathered over a period of time. The portfolio provides evidence of performance in each unit and element of competence required to do the job satisfactorily.

There are many other ways that S/NVQs may be used for development purposes. You may be able to use them as a way of establishing standards in:

* selection and recruitment
* induction
* appraisal
* job analysis
* training needs analysis.

If you want to know more about S/NVQs, contact your local Training and Enterprise Council and ask to speak to the person responsible for NVQs. You may find that you not only get useful advice but in many cases there may be a scheme to subsidize the cost of training and assessment leading to NVQs.

You can also contact:

National Council for Vocational Qualifications (NCVQ)
222 Euston Road
London NW1 2EF
Tel: 0171 387 9898

(The NCVQ is due to merge with the School Curriculum and Assessment Authority and will be called the Qualifications and National Curriculum Authority.)

For information about supervisor and management awards you should approach:

Management Charter Initiative
Russell Square House
Russell Square
London WC1B 5AE
Telephone: 0171 872 9000

The Management Charter Initiative is an independent body set up by employers and backed by the Government with the aim of improving the performance of the UK's managers. Materials and publications are provided to cover the different arrangements and levels.

The benefits of going down the NVQ route are that you are conforming to agreed national standards and giving your employees a chance to achieve qualifications which they can accumulate at stages over a period of time. They may be able to get recognition for existing competences without any extra training. They will, however, need guidance on how to prepare for NVQ assessment.

Some employers, on the other hand, have found that they prefer to use their own schemes of training and assessment. Preparing for assessment can also prove a rather protracted and difficult process for some employees.

How, as a manager, can you reduce the risk of choosing the wrong course?

Think back for a moment to your own experience of choosing courses and workshops that you wanted to attend. You may feel that there was an element of luck for you as a participant in how successful a choice you made. If you were fortunate, the various steps outlined in the list on pp. 71–2 above were taken by you or your manager and these should have helped ensure a good outcome.

When you now find yourself allocating your own training budget to send people on events, you will be particularly keen to reduce the risk of wasting nominations to courses, for whatever reason.

Use your networks

If you work in an organization which has a training department or a trainer, see if they have already used a particular supplier. Ask for their opinion. They should be able to provide some evidence to back it up. It is a good idea to keep evaluation information and share it with colleagues who may be looking for similar training.

Seek suggestions from other managers whose judgement you trust. They may have some invaluable information to share on successful courses.

Ask the course provider if you can speak to any purchasers. Again ask their opinion, but remember that you will have inevitably been directed to those who thought that the event was generally successful. In using any evaluative comment of this sort you have to bear in mind also that what is good for one individual may not be so good for another. However, the broad picture should be useful and a third party does not usually have anything to lose by being frank. Another suggestion is to sample one workshop or course before committing to a whole programme.

Evaluate any published materials that the course provider makes available. In particular, what should you look for when you assess a course or workshop programme? Table 5.1 shows a sample programme. The notes in the margins draw attention to some key features that you should look for.

Table 5.1   SAMPLE PROGRAMME

	Developing personal effectiveness
	Rationale
There should be some general statement, like this, to give you an idea about the trainer's rationale.	*This workshop is designed for staff who wish to explore and develop their potential to be more effective at work. The focus is on examining current personal skills, style and strengths to identify future personal development issues. These can then be developed and integrated in a practical and realistic way back in the workplace. It also provides an opportunity for participants to evaluate their current career path and scope for future personal development.*
	Target group
Check this to see if it fits your learners.	*This workshop is intended for staff in non-management positions.*

This tells you what the trainer hopes to achieve in running the event.

Aim

It is designed to enable participants to assess and improve their personal performance at work.

These objectives should give you a clear view of what your learners will know and be able to do, after the event.

Objectives

By the end of the workshop participants will have worked to achieve the following outcomes:

- *analyse their own personal skills and strengths in working effectively;*
- *increase their awareness of the causes of stress in both organizations and individuals and ways of coping, preventing or confronting it;*
- *improve their use of time;*
- *improve planning for short-term and long-term developments by setting objectives and action plans.*

Check to see that there are not more than five objectives. Beyond that they become less useful.

This tells you about the chosen style and approaches.

Training approach

We plan to involve both the participant and their manager in some pre- and post-course work and discussion. This is important to encourage shared responsibility and communication about the participant's development and this should benefit both the individual and the organization in the future.

Our training style aims to create a confidential and safe environment where participants are encouraged to discuss personal issues openly with others. Through the effective facilitation of group discussion and a strong emphasis on active participation in practical exercises within the programme, it is hoped that participants will take responsibility for their own future personal development.

In order to achieve significant commit-

ment to change and growth we will encourage participants to experiment with various techniques for sustaining and continuing the process of the course over the subsequent weeks and months. These will include documented action planning with the support of managers, networking with other participants and the maintenance of a learning log.

Method of delivery

A variety of training methods will be incorporated to encourage the effective development of knowledge and skills. The methods used include theory input, small-group discussion, structured exercises including role plays, case studies and pre-course questionnaires.

This gives you some idea of what the event will be like for participants, in this case, not all lectures.

Course participants

The ideal number of participants for this course is 8–10 to allow one tutor to present and manage the practical exercises effectively. However, two tutors could be used for a larger group of about 14–16 participants. They could then share input and work more intensively by facilitating discussion in two small groups throughout all the practical exercises.

If you were commissioning this workshop for your staff, you would need to take this recommendation seriously.

Two tutors will probably double the cost, though.

Outline programme

Day 1. Steps to greater personal effectiveness.

- *Introduction – review of objectives and ground rule setting*
- *Assessing your own personal effectiveness*
- *What stops you being more effective?*
- *Dividing jobs into manageable activities*
- *Working with others more effectively*
- *Clearer communications*
- *Managing time within given schedules*
- *Learning from crises and failures*

You might feel you need more information about content and timings. Ask the trainer.

An important opening discussion

It is always useful to do this.

The trainer recognizes the need to help people think their way back into the course.

There is an expectation that some 'action' will result from the course.

Ask to see a blank evaluation form. Confirm that you will see all the completed forms at the end of the event.

● *Handling stress*
● *Review of learning points for day 1.*

Day 2. Practice for greater effectiveness

● *Re-engagement activity*
● *Working on prepared scenarios:*
  – Practice in analysing work-loads and priorities
  – Practice in planning the use of time
  – Practice in communications skills for greater effectiveness
  – Practice in creating more effective working relations
● *Action planning*
● *Course evaluation.*

In-house or external providers?

Only managers who work in an organization that has its own training unit have a choice of in-house or external providers. In such situations how do you choose?

You may have no choice, if the learning need is very specialized or carries some special accreditation. For example, if you want to help someone to prepare for the role of company secretary, they will almost certainly need to enrol with the nearest centre providing an award-bearing course accredited by the Institute of Chartered Secretaries and Administrators.

Alternatively there may be training which is specifically geared to the business plan and working environment of your organization, and this will have to be provided by you or your trainers, or an external provider selected and brought in by you or your trainers.

If you have a choice between more or less similar offerings in-house and externally, you may be swayed towards the in-house choice by the following factors:

● the possibility of lower costs;
● relevance to your work setting;
● negligible travel and subsistence costs;
● the accountability of your training unit.

Weigh up very carefully the benefits of generic training workshops run by external providers on such topics as how to negotiate, being assertive, managing difficult people. They may have an inspirational quality and provide an opportunity for your staff to meet and share ideas with people from other organizations. They may also have a social benefit for your people, particularly if the event is held in a pleasant setting.

However, you cannot normally expect this sort of training to do much more than identify general problems and offer general solutions. The cheaper end of the market tends towards the 'pile 'em high', mass-produced type of training, rolled off the line by skilled operators. But you pays your money and takes your choice.

Choosing and using a trainer

In some circumstances, particularly in smaller companies and organizations, you may decide that the most effective way of meeting the needs of a group of staff is to approach an external trainer and commission them to come in and provide the training for you.

Here is a checklist that will guide you through the process.

1   *Produce a written brief or think through your answers on these points.*   An external trainer will want to ask questions on:
     • the title of the training;
     • who is to be trained;
     • why the need has arisen;
     • what you aim to achieve through commissioning the training;
     • what you want learners to be able to know and do after the training;
     • an indication of dates for the events and the number of repeats, if any;
     • how much the training will cost, including fees and expenses;

- whom to contact for a fuller discussion of the brief, if necessary.

2 *Find suitable trainers.* All the processes already described for finding an external provider apply. Approach more than one and ask for a written proposal. You may have to ask for tenders in a public-sector organization. In any event, if you have time, approach a couple of likely providers but explain to them that you are doing so.

3 *Allow time to talk your brief through with potential providers.* If you are asking them to travel and spend significant amounts of time preparing a proposal, be ready for the possibility of their asking for some expenses or a fee. You, of course, decide whether you will get a better result by paying it.

4 *Assess the proposals carefully.* Look for the same features that have been outlined earlier in this chapter in the sample programme.

5 *Written agreement.* Having chosen your trainer, agree in writing the main terms of the job and also agree what will happen in the event that you have to postpone or cancel. Most trainers will have terms of business which are designed to place the responsibility and the cost on you, if you cancel at the last minute.

6 *Check the domestic arrangements.* Make sure that all the administrative arrangements are in place for the day or days, including tea, coffee and lunch-time breaks.

7 *Point of contact.* Give clear instructions on how the trainer can contact you or your nominated colleague on arrival.

8 *Keeping in touch.* Suggest to the trainer that you introduce the event briefly, so that learners realize you give it your full support. Show your face unobtrusively at lunch-time and/or at the end of the day. You can get a good feel for the way the event has been received. The trainer may also have information that they want to share with you.

9 *Evaluation.* Look through the evaluation sheets and talk to learners after the event.

10 *Tidy up.* Make sure that participants' records are

updated. Decide whether you will use this trainer again. Assuming you are happy with the service, pay the trainer promptly on receipt of their invoice. If not, discuss any problems and negotiate a reduced fee.

In the next chapter you can read about how to get the best out of the training you have chosen.

Summary

Having read this chapter you should have been encouraged to think about the way you choose the training events your staff attend. You started this process by reflecting on your own experience of training events. Then you reviewed three common types of training events. You were provided with some information sources for finding out about what training is available. If the idea of accreditation and S/NVQs was unfamiliar to you, you now have some initial understanding and an address to use for further information.

Judging the quality of training events is essential, if you are not to waste valuable opportunities and resources. You were given some guidelines on what to look for. Finally, you considered a checklist to help you select a trainer should you decide to invite one to run an event for you.

Reading on

Fletcher, S. (1994), *NVQs Standards and Competence*, 2nd edn, London: Kogan Page. (A comprehensive and authoritative guide to the development and application of National Vocational Qualifications.)

■ 6

Getting the best out of training events

In the last chapter you considered how to choose training events. Once you have made your choice, you will want to ensure that both your organization and the employee get the best out of training workshops and courses. You might be tempted to think that once you have chosen a training event for and with your member of staff, that is it. However, by spending a little time before and after the event on preparing and following up, you can increase the benefits your staff will gain from attending.

The aim of this chapter is to equip you to plan individual and group attendance at training events so that your staff learn in a purposeful way. To achieve this you will be asked to:

- *plan how to prepare staff for the selected course or workshop;*
- *check their expectations;*
- *follow up the event by checking on their views, assessing what they learned and helping ensure that it is not wasted.*

These are the topics you will be reading more about:

- *how to help staff benefit from training events;*
- *your rights as a purchaser of training;*
- *planning to choose and use your next training event.*

How to help staff benefit from training events

In order to maximize the benefits you need to focus on three areas.

1   Ensure that your nominated staff member is prepared for the event – have you taken the time and effort beforehand to discuss it with them and establish their commitment to attending and learning?

2   Ensure that in longer courses consisting of a number of events over a period of time the learner has enough support to make the programme work – you, as a manager, should take regular interest in progress. You may also encourage the learner to choose and work with a mentor in or outside your organization. There is more on mentoring in the next chapter.

3   Follow up after the training event – have you scheduled time to talk over the event with the participant and ensured that there are immediate opportunities for learning to be applied and used in the workplace?

Failure to do one or all of these will reduce the value of the event.

Preparation

Here is a checklist for establishing a working contract with your staff member before they go on a course.

1   Who initiated the idea of going? Was it you, the organization or your member of staff? If it was you or the organization, you will need to check the following points.

    • *Do they understand your reason for suggesting it?* This will be far easier if you have already established a training and development plan with them. The plan may have been developed during an appraisal interview; or this may have been done as part of their induction to the organization. Then the proposed course can be shown to fit into this plan.

    It is a much harder and potentially fruitless job to 'send' someone on a course, without revealing to them that you have a development aim in mind. Then the proposition is seen as a covert criticism and the motivation to go will be dampened or destroyed.

- *Do they understand the aims and objectives of the course?* The easiest way is to talk these through and ask if the aims and objectives cover the sort of skills and knowledge the learner wants to acquire.
- *Do they know what you have done to check its suitability for them?* You can show what value you attach to the event by explaining what you have done to confirm that the course will be useful and interesting for them. Your enthusiasm and positive expectations will provide a model for the learner.

  Invite the learner to share any concerns they may have about any aspect of going on the course. If it is residential, for example, a person who has not frequently attended such events may be concerned about potential conflict with family responsibilities. They may have these worries so much to the fore of their mind that they will not fully commit to the course. Talk them through and see if you can help them find solutions.

  If it is the organization that requires attendance at an event, check all the points above. You will also have to show that you support the idea and are expecting the event be worth backing.

  If you dissociate yourself from the idea and they also do not want to go, it is probably a waste of time to proceed. If you really question the value of sending the person on the course, the responsible line as a manager is to take it up with your line manager; do not dump the problem on the learner. Saying nothing is weak management and will be seen as such by the member of staff. 'My manager knows it will be a waste of time but has not got the guts to say so.'

2 If they initiated the idea of going, you will need to make sure of the following.
  - *Is their motivation still strong?* Encourage them to say what expectations they have and to explain how they hope the course will be of use to them and you.
  - *Is the course's purpose fully understood?* Go through the programme with them, if you are in doubt.
  - *Are there any practical or social barriers to overcome?*

Finally, once you are committed to their going, do not under any circumstances pester them with phone calls during the day or, even worse, call them back. Either the training event is worth doing or it is not; do not confuse matters by intervening.

Checking expectations

Try a pre-course activity with your nominated member of staff. Ask them to list their objectives in joining the course and then add your own expectations. Discuss what you have both written and, with their consent, send the form to the course provider before the event.

During a development programme

Learners on longer courses or development programmes will almost inevitably run into difficulties somewhere down the line.

Here are just some of the reasons. They may:

- experience lack of motivation;
- have domestic difficulties which hinder progress;
- find the course too basic, too difficult or in other ways inappropriate to their needs;
- lose confidence in the lecturer or trainer running the programme.

So, as their manager, you should not agree to their joining a course or programme unless you are prepared to take some continuing interest in their progress.

There are different levels of interest, though. You must decide what is appropriate for you and them. You may be far too busy to become a coach or alternative tutor. The course may be on a particular specialism that you yourself are not familiar with.

You might consider helping the learner choose a mentor. This would be someone who is not directly responsible for them as a manager. A mentor needs to agree with the learner how much time they can give and what type of help they can offer. It may be that the learner needs technical expertise, a sympathetic ear or an independent sounding-board. There is more on the mentor role in the next chapter.

You should continue to take an interest in the learner's progress. In particular, discuss with them how what they are learning may be applied in the workplace.

Follow-up

After a training event make sure that the benefit of the course or workshop is not lost. Sometimes learners are subjected to a re-entry ritual by their more inflexible colleagues. The usual refrain is, 'You can forget all that rubbish; it doesn't work here!'.

Simply having an informal conversation with the learner on their return will show some recognition that it was worth their going. A more structured response would ask the learner to:

- produce a short report to share with colleagues;
- share the key learning points at a team meeting;
- draw up some recommendations on how to implement changes that they have learnt about on the course;
- tell you in what ways they want to change their role or function now that they have finished the course;
- say what they would like to train in next, when the opportunity arises.

Your rights as a purchaser of training

If you do not feel that your member of staff received the quality of training that you and they expected, you should take this up with the training provider. Be careful to discuss the problem thoroughly with your member of staff, so that you can gather solid evidence about ways in which the event failed, and refer to the brochure on which you based your decision to buy. Are there any guarantees or conditions which were part of the offer?

Here is a checklist of indicators you might use when deciding whether to seek a refund for a training event.

- The pre-course material was misleading about the purpose and target group of the course.
- The course materials were inaccurate or incomplete.
- The celebrity presenter featured on the programme was replaced by a less experienced presenter who showed signs of not knowing the material thoroughly.
- One or more of the objectives were not met.
- A significant part of the programme was not covered and this omission was not discussed and negotiated with participants.
- Additional material was included which did not relate to the declared objectives.
- The environment for the event was not conducive to learning (too hot, too cold, too noisy or uncomfortable).

Any responsible training provider should take your complaint seriously, provided it is supported by evidence of the sort listed above. You can usually negotiate some redress, for example a voucher for a further course, or a refund. It helps, though, if you have checked the terms and conditions in the brochure when you booked.

Planning to choose and use your next training event

Use what you have learnt during this chapter when you next select a training event for a member of your staff. The following checklist summarizes the steps.

1   *The learner.*
   - Their defined training need
   - What do you as the manager want from the event?
   - What does the learner want from the event?
   - How does the event fit into the learner's development programme?

2 *Choosing a training event.*
  - Which networks will you use within and outside the organization?
  - Will you use your training department's database? If so, whom will you contact?
  - Will you use local information sources and databases? If so, which ones?
3 *Vetting what is on offer.*
  - Which is the most informative published programme?
  - Who can be most helpful in giving an opinion on the course?
  - How useful are providers in giving further information on their courses?
4 *Choosing your provider.* Have you considered all the options:
  - in-house trainers;
  - external courses;
  - in-house events commissioned from external trainers?
5 *Accreditation and NVQs.* Are they:
  - important to you;
  - important to the learner?
6 *Before the event.*
  - Have you used the pre-course form suggested in this chapter or something of your own making which achieves the same result?
7 *During longer programmes.*
  - Have you planned how you will keep in touch with the learner's progress?
  - Have you discussed with your learner the usefulness of having a mentor?
8 *Follow-up.*
  - How will you ensure that the effort and cost involved in the course are a real benefit to the learner, to you and to the organization?

Summary

You have considered what you need to do as a manager to ensure that your staff derive full benefit from attending training courses: you should prepare them and check both their and your expectations. You also considered what your role should be in supporting participants on longer courses, and how, at the end of a course (whether short or long), you should follow up.

You were given a checklist of reasons for seeking a refund for a training event.

The chapter concluded with a checklist to help you choose and use your next training event.

Reading on

Rae, L. (1997), *How to Measure Training Effectiveness*, 3rd edn, Aldershot: Gower. (Covers the process of selection and planning of training events.)

■ 7

Developing your staff as they work

In Chapter 1 you considered ways in which people learn at work. The learning process is going on all the time. Sometimes it is positive and constructive and sometimes it is the opposite. In this chapter you are asked to focus on the deliberate steps that you can take to help an employee develop in ways which are of benefit to you as their manager, to the organization and, of course, to them.

The principles which lie behind these approaches are to do with giving staff greater responsibility and independence to learn. In deciding to look systematically for learning opportunities for your staff, you yourself will be making changes to your management approach and learning more about how you relate to your staff and the work of the department.

Many of the ideas in this chapter can be very easily introduced into your work setting. Indeed, it is quite likely that you are already doing some of them. If this is so, ask yourself how fully you are exploiting the learning potential of the particular approach. Have you explained to the employee how a different way of working might open up new possibilities and help them develop new skills? The processes and skills which you will use in doing these things draw heavily on what you have read in Chapter 2, 'Helping people learn at work'. For example, if you are a good listener or you have developed your skill in giving and receiving feedback, you will find that many of the ideas you are now going to consider are well within your scope to act on with your work group.

The aim of this chapter is to help you to understand how managers can help their staff use the day-to-day experience of work as a means of developing their effectiveness. You will also make some choices about which methods you can use with your own staff. To achieve this you will be asked to:

- *identify the development opportunities in assigning, managing and reviewing work;*
- *consider the range of working relations and tasks which offer scope for learning;*
- *plan how you will design and manage developmental assignments for your employees;*
- *learn how you and they can get most value out of work-based training and development.*

These are the topics you will be reading more about:

- *planning for day-to-day support;*
- *finding development opportunities within work;*
- *acting up, or temporary promotion;*
- *Action Learning;*
- *coaching;*
- *delegation;*
- *instruction and demonstration;*
- *mentoring;*
- *project work;*
- *work shadowing.*

Planning for day-to-day support

As you work together with your staff each day you build up a profile of their behaviour and competence at work. (Of course they are also doing the same for you as their manager.) You can use this information to help develop individual performance. In any interaction you have which is designed to have development outcomes, you will be using the key ideas about the learning process which were covered in Chapter 1, 'How people learn at work' and Chapter 2, 'Helping people learn at work'.

Different members of your work group need different levels and types of support on a day-to-day basis. Some are well established in their posts and you have learnt to give them space and independence to get on with the job. Their results are normally on or above target, and when occasionally they are not you always find that they can explain why. With such people there is the risk of taking their performance for granted. They may need new challenges, or they may simply need a bit more of your interest and positive feedback from time to time.

You will also have less experienced staff who may be new to the organization or new to their particular post. The frequency of your interventions will need to be greater. As you assign work to them you will want to specify objectives clearly and check that they have understood and know how to complete the task to the required standard. When that particular job is completed you will take the opportunity to review with them the quality and completeness of the work. This sort of discussion provides a very good opportunity to talk with them about the experience of doing the job and to identify what they have learnt from it.

You will also have staff whose performance has declined. This management challenge was discussed in Chapter 3, 'Improving performance'. There you read that there are many reasons for poor performance but that it is up to you to take some action either to achieve the necessary change or take a broader view of the person's suitability for the job.

Whichever of these types of day-to-day working relationships you manage during the coming weeks, have the following framework of questions in mind as you assign some piece of work or oversee some continuing activity. Use the checklist as your prompt. Assess the needs of the individual and the complexity of the job and decide how to apply those questions that fit the circumstances. In approaching development discussions of this sort, bear in mind what you have read about helping people learn in Chapter 2. It is no good conducting a review in such a way that you undermine confidence or confirm feelings of inadequacy.

Preparing to assign a piece of work

In assigning this piece of work, check in your own mind the following questions:

1 Has the employee sufficient experience and skill to do the task? If not, find some coaching/training for them to

complete before starting or to have available when they need it.

2   From your knowledge of their past performance, where are they going to have difficulties? Plan to discuss these before they arise and ask the employee how they can be reduced.

3   What would they like you to do to help?

4   What would they like others to do?

5   Have you discussed and set performance objectives for the work and are they SMART? (See Chapter 3, 'Improving performance', page 48 for a reminder of what the acronym SMART means.)

6   Have you agreed some learning objectives which may match what you have already found out about skills or past performance gaps? Often it will be most helpful to work on one learning need at a time so that the employee can focus on improving it and you can measure how far they do so.

During the work

1   Have you checked at appropriate intervals on progress towards both performance and learning objectives? As we have already noted, the frequency of this will vary according to the independence and experience of the employee.

2   Are any arrangements for coaching and other forms of support proving to be effective? For example, if you arranged attendance at an open learning centre so that your employee could learn how to use a new software package, are they happy working like this and is the service that the centre provides satisfactory?

After the work

1   Was the work on time and to standard?

2   Were all the objectives met?

3   Were there aspects of the work which posed unforeseen problems?

4   Has the learner learnt something about the way of doing

this job which they can use in the future or that you could use in managing it with them or with others?

5 Have they learnt something more generally about how they respond when, for example, they do not know some key information or lack a particular skill?
6 How do they cope with setbacks in completing the task?
7 How do they respond to negative feedback from others?
8 How good are they at asserting their rights, for example at saying 'no' to unreasonable demands from others, or from you?
9 What have they learnt from the success of the job?
10 How has this helped them in preparing for a similar or tougher assignment?
11 Do they now realize that they have a development need in a particular area, and what can they and you do to find a solution?

Remember, it is not suggested that you will need formally to ask all these questions every time you assign a task. Rather, it should become natural for you to make mature judgements about the fit between the person and the job and always be looking for the development opportunities that each occasion presents.

Finding development opportunities within work

Development opportunities within work present themselves continually. You need to develop a mind set which helps you identify them – 'That went well; why did it and what can we learn from it?'; 'That was a near-disaster; we must find out why and learn how to prevent it happening again'. Start by modelling the process in the way you manage the staff you have most immediate contact with. You need to create trust and be consistent in showing that you want to help people become more effective at work. Spread the word and support it by example. If you feel that there is some lack of trust, work first with those who are positively inclined to change. Feature your ideas when you have performance-related conversations with your staff, whether in formal appraisal reviews or at the beginning or end of an assignment. A good opener might be, 'What can I do to help you learn more about this? How can we make sure that you have some practice so that you do this better?'

Your goal should be to foster a climate at work which supports learning and creates opportunities. People should talk about training and development projects you have helped them formulate. Successful outcomes should be featured and celebrated. Most critically, you need to be seen to be consistent in your offer, not just a fair-weather innovator. This means accepting that mistakes provide an opportunity to learn.

The main reason for this emphasis on learning is that, without it, the organization will lose ground against competitors. Unless everyone is looking for ways of doing things better and regarding this as a normal and perpetual process, other more innovative and effective organizations will take the work from you.

The development opportunities which follow in this chapter have been arranged in alphabetical order for ease of reference.

Acting up, or temporary promotion

Acting up means asking someone to fill a vacancy on a temporary basis. Why do this rather than fill the vacancy permanently? If you have the choice, fill the vacancy as a matter of course. There will be justifiable concern among employees if too many vacancies are covered temporarily or if the period of acting up is extended for the wrong reasons – for example, to put off the effort involved in finding a suitable replacement. However, some vacancies are very hard to fill in a hurry. Some occur very abruptly and some functions are so vital to the success of your operation that you cannot possibly leave them unassigned for the three to six months that it will often take to recruit a new jobholder.

There are important development opportunities in arranging for a suitably experienced employee, or small group of employees, to take over on a temporary basis some or all of the responsibilities of the person leaving.

If the experience is to have any lasting value for the staff member, you will have to spend some time inducting them to the new role and monitoring their performance. You should also make sure that a record of their new duties is kept. Their progress in this temporary position should be reviewed, assessed and recorded when it is completed during a performance appraisal intervie.

The learning opportunities in acting up

As a manager, you can see how well a person rises to the challenge. They may reveal skills, knowledge and attitudes that you never suspected they had. Assess the extent to which they are energized by the change. How do they cope with the inevitable difficulties of moving at short notice into a new role and responsibilities? How far do they share their ups and downs openly with you? If they are trying too hard to deny any difficulties, ask yourself what you can do to create a more open, no-blame climate in this relationship. Perhaps not revealing their hand is an indication that they are really out of their depth, so be ready to talk this through and encourage more open dialogue.

For many members of staff, acting up has much to offer. As more organizations change to flatter management structures there are fewer promotion opportunities. Other ways have to be found to extend and challenge staff. Acting up may give you a way of doing this. In their new temporary post, staff who are acting up will learn a lot about their own capacities and confidence. Provided you have made a reasonable choice in your candidate, they will thrive on the challenge.

How to make it work

You, as their manager, must make sure that the placement in the temporary post works. You will have to weigh up the longer-term benefits against the option of filling the vacancy as quickly as possible.

An important question for both you and the temporary appointee is what to do when the period of acting up comes to an end. One outcome of a very successful temporary post may be that you no longer need to look for an external candidate because you have grown one of your own. You may have to check with your personnel department, if you have one, to see whether, in order to meet your personnel and equal opportunities policy requirements, you should still put the vacancy up for genuine competition. If you do, you can then test your judgement by measuring your internal candidate fairly, along with other applicants.

If the temporary post-holder is not to be considered for a permanent position, you will need to plan together how to ensure that all the benefits of the new work experience are not lost. You may choose to:

- offer a different assignment which more closely suits the new expertise of the temporary jobholder (depending, in part, on the flexibility and size of your organizational structure);
- explore with the post-holder how they can apply what they have learnt to improve their old job;
- explain that you want them to return to their existing post, but that you are actively looking for a new opening for them when the opportunity arises – the more precise you can be, the more likely they are to have confidence in your intentions.

Action Learning

Action Learning sets are a common feature in organizations which value staff development. The idea of Action Learning was first developed by management writer and consultant Reg Revans (Revans, 1979). Action Learning is designed to convert the actions of your daily engagement in work into learning opportunities. This is done by a process of reflection and mutual support between members of an Action Learning set.

The opportunities in Action Learning

It is argued that employees learn better from each other when dealing with real problems than they do by attending courses. Action Learning puts the focus on development by creating an expectation that the organization can only grow and change if its managers and staff are committed to learning together. Once unleashed, the learning process may change the organizational environment. In most cases this will be no disadvantage. There is some cost in providing facilitation and meeting time for the Action Learning set, but this should be more than recompensed by the increased commitment to learning by acting, reflecting and planning improved performance.

What does it take to get Action Learning going?

The most important place to start is with the group who may form the Action Learning set. Focus on the issues and tasks that most concern them as a group, for example how to improve productivity or quality of service, or how to achieve a more positive and motivated workforce. Talk over your intentions. Agree to work on one of these issues as a priority and to do so as an Action Learning group, meeting at intervals to share experiences and agree objectives for further action. It is probable that you will need someone to help the Action Learning set form and develop. You may do this yourself but your management role may make this problematic on occasions. An important principle of Action Learning is that the set should be open to all ideas of its constituent members and some staff may feel this will be inhibited by the presence of their manager.

A learning group has to generate and use its own ground rules and manage the changing dynamic of its membership. The vacuum created in an apparently leaderless group will soon be filled, and this may not be to the advantage of the group if it is dominated by one or two powerful individuals. It is likely then that you will need a facilitator who brings no personal 'baggage'.

Speak to your training department if you have one, and see if they can provide someone to act as a facilitator to work with your Action Learning set or sets, particularly as it establishes itself and defines its purpose and method of working. If you do not have such a resource in-house, find it from an external provider. You may already have used a local training company. Talk your plans over with them and see what experience they have had in working with Action Learning sets. If you have no such contacts, speak to your local Training and Enterprise Council or Business Link, or try the business school of your local university or college.

Coaching

What is meant by coaching in the context of training and development? Coaching can be described as helping or enabling an individual in the workplace, or a small group, to acquire knowledge or develop a skill or skills which are needed to improve job performance. Coaching is something we all do informally from time to time when someone scratches their head and says, 'I'm completely stuck trying to do this; can you help?'.

A comparison might be made with a sports coach, who helps individuals or teams perform better in a game. You would expect a coach to have demonstrated competence at the particular sport. This would give them credibility and show that they were not making it up as they went along. Coaching is particularly important for novices, young or old, entering a sport for the first time. The help at this level may be a series of one-hour classes for a group. It is possible for a parent or friend to provide coaching.

Sports people heading towards professional status still need coaching, but at a more sophisticated level. Some of the work that sports coaches do is skills based. They show what techniques and methods are needed to improve the swing, the jump, the throw. They try to help people develop tactics and also take a more strategic view of the match or the game. The coaching relationship allows coach and player to review and work on behavioural issues. A good coach instils confidence and determination. They help set goals and provide feedback and support.

The learning opportunities in coaching

Most of what has just been identified as good coaching in a sports setting can be applied to the way you coach your staff, even if some of the more competitive sporting values would need to be reframed to be useful at work, for example competing with your own best previous performance rather then defeating a colleague!

Although coaching may come naturally to many people, the coaching invitation, 'Can you help me?', may trigger in some managers or colleagues a desire to point score or dominate. This sort of response will kill off the learning relationship in minutes. 'I'm not asking them for help again; they made me feel stupid.' If coaching is done badly, this aspect of your development plan will fall into discredit. It therefore needs to be backed up by training in coaching skills.

Who should coach?

In a work setting you may be the best person to coach some of your staff from time to time, but you are unlikely to have either the energy or the time to do it for all of them. So, in encouraging coaching, consider ways of making it part of the accepted practice for all managers and supervisors in your work group or organization.

This proposition may cause you to throw up your hands in horror: how will X or Y ever manage to coach? Indeed, you yourself may in your more honest moments wonder how you would coach certain individuals who are resistant to being managed, let alone being helped to learn. Work at these two blockages. Maybe part of the reason why individuals can be difficult from time to time is because they do not feel valued by you or by the organization. Coaching may provide an opportunity either to show to the resistors that you care about their development, if you are the coach, or that you value their expertise, if you want them to coach others. In any event it will take some preparation and training to get the necessary skills and quality of coaching relationship that are needed.

You can use coaching for skills development, such as setting up a machine; performance development, such as meeting an agreed standard in responding to customer enquiries; or behavioural development, such as better time management.

Your aim should be to create an environment where coaching is a natural first option which managers and others turn to in trying to meet a learning need.

How to get started on coaching

Give your work group practical examples of coaching which they can use as a model. Encourage others to see coaching as part of their management or supervisory function. Ask people to offer help to others. Incorporate some coaching into the induction programme for new staff. Consider running some training with a title such as 'Coaching skills or Helping people to learn'. Chapter 10, 'Planning a training event' and Chapter 11, 'Delivering a training event' will provide you with the practical training skills to do this. If you do not feel ready to try this yet, ask a trainer who knows your type of work to prepare and provide a programme for you.

Coaching skills

The skills you should develop to become a good coach are no different from those that you need to help people learn in other types of development activity. They include:

- listening skills, to establish what the learner already knows and how motivated they are to learn;
- facilitation skills, to help keep the focus on the learner so that *they* do the work and you support them, rather than tell them all the answers or belabour them with advice;
- instructional skills, to make clear presentations and demonstrations on how to perform tasks;
- feedback skills, to enable the learner to develop their own

sense of how well they are doing – this includes praising wherever it is justified;

- challenging, to help the learner reassess performance;
- assessing skills, to test understanding and performance.

There is further guidance on these skills, later in this chapter and in Chapter 2, 'Helping people learn at work'.

Delegation

Consider the benefits to you if you can systematically and effectively delegate some of your work. It is most unlikely that you are underemployed; but there is a difference between 'busy' and 'downright overworked'. In some organizations managers are made to feel they have to be on the verge of collapse through overload to prove their worth. It need not be like that; in fact it is almost certainly unproductive for it to be like that. It is of course possible that you have chosen to work in an environment where you can only achieve grace through self-punishment! If you are really carrying an excessive load single-handed, your own manager should be considering redesigning the work and matching the appropriate staffing to the tasks.

If you actually think that a consistent diet of overworking is self-fulfilling, switch to another book now and take out comprehensive health insurance. If you do not like working in this way, face up to the fact that you have to have an assertive conversation with your manager. Say how you feel and what effect it is having on your work and on you as a person. Failing all else, think of looking for a new organization to work for, where more sense prevails.

The other avenue to explore is to ask yourself why you are not delegating more effectively.

The learning opportunities in delegating

Delegation is a key management process. It will make your own work routines more manageable and increase the productivity of your work group. It also creates excellent opportunities for you to provide structured learning for your staff. Some functions can be delegated on a continuing basis. Where this is the sensible choice, your responsibility is to monitor the performance of the person concerned from time to time and see how they are managing the task. In appraisal interviews, and indeed whenever the opportunity arises, you can give feedback on the way you see the delegated task working out. Do not give the impression that you have dumped the task on the employee and lost interest. Another possibility is to rotate the delegation of routine tasks, so that a number of people get the opportunity to demonstrate how they perform. Each person will have their own skills and talents to bring to the job.

Other delegation opportunities arise when there is a new project or special assignment to be tackled.

How to delegate effectively

When you have identified a task or project that you need to delegate, first of all consider what competences are needed to complete it to the required standard. Ask yourself what knowledge and skills you need when you do it.

Next, think through your work group and see who has the best match of competences. They do not necessarily need to have them all. You may decide that this will be a very good development opportunity for an individual, provided you or another competent person can provide some coaching to supplement what they can already do.

Most importantly, be clear in your mind before going into the delegation what level of authority you are prepared to hand over. It will be very damaging to your relationship with the delegatee if you delegate and then withdraw the task because it has gone wrong.

It is usual to choose one of the following levels of delegation.

1   The delegatee has a free hand to complete the task to meet agreed objectives and standards. You will not require them to consult with you until the work is completed, if then.

2   The delegatee prepares their own plan and does the work. They will report during the work, only by exception, if an unforeseen obstacle or problem has arisen.
3   Before starting, the delegatee agrees a plan with you, and also agrees key stages when progress will be reviewed.
4   The choice of which level will depend on the complexity and duration of the work and the experience and competence of the delegatee.

Draw up a clear agreement or contract before the task begins. Let others know what you have asked the delegatee to do. At the end of the task, make sure that you discuss the learning outcomes of the activity. What has the delegatee learnt about their present level of competence? Where do they and you need to plan further training and development? Use the opportunity to praise them for the success and say how much you appreciated being able to leave the task in their hands.

Instruction and demonstration

There are some learning needs which can be sensibly met only by instruction and demonstration. Instruction involves telling, showing, practice and feedback. Some typical situations where this would be a good way to help someone learn might be:

- replacing a toner cartridge in a printer or copier;
- handling a tool or a process safely;
- giving an injection;
- using a formula to calculate some results;
- creating a database;
- learning the features of a new piece of equipment.

Instruction and demonstration may well form part of the coaching relationship. You might also use these skills in running a group training session. There is more on this in Chapter 11, 'Delivering a training event'.

The learning opportunities in instruction and demonstration

Provided you use some basic rules listed below, instruction and demonstration may be the only way to transfer some types of knowledge and skills. The alternative may be trial and error but this can be wasteful, demotivating and possibly dangerous in some situations. There is also an additional learning opportunity in instruction in that you have a chance to get to know the individual or group you are working with, as learners and people. They also get to know you. They will for example identify how patient you are and how interested in their learning.

Although it is obviously possible to instruct simply by talking, it would be perverse not to use some form of demonstration in most work-based instruction, even if it is in the form of a simulation or via some learning material such as a video. Follow this up by setting up a period of experiment and practice for the learner. Ask the learner to assess their own performance. You will also need to conclude the process by giving your own feedback.

Some basic rules of instruction and demonstration

1   Prepare for your piece of instruction.
    • Work through the activity which is to be learnt.
    • Decide on the learning objectives you plan to meet in the session.
    • Divide the activity up into its main stages.
    • Identify the reasons why one step needs to follow the other.
    • Identify any general processes that the learner will need to understand and use to complete the task.
    • Prepare any overview diagrams, checklists, plans or detailed reference material that will help the learner.
2   Check what your learners already know before you start.
3   Explain the learning objectives you hope they will meet; for example, 'By the end of this session you should be

able to plan how to move a patient from a chair to a wheelchair safely without injuring your back'.

4   Discuss what evidence you will be looking for in assessing whether they have met the objectives. (It may be that there is already a set of competences drawn up for this particular part of the job. If so, use these.)

5   Explain the sequence of the material to be covered. Then explain that you are starting with the first part.

6   As you complete each part, recap the main points and ask if the learner has any questions.

7   Build in opportunities to test understanding by short practice sessions or question and answer tests.

8   In demonstrating processes and skills, reduce distractions and unnecessary detail to a minimum. Work at a speed that suits the learner.

9   At the end of the session go over the main learning points, take any final questions, then run a short test activity to measure how well the objectives have been attained.

10   Provide further instruction and practice on aspects that are still unclear.

In general, remember to say what you are about to say, say it and then remind the learner what has been said. Pay attention to the learner's responses to check that they are interested and engaged in the subject. Use questions to encourage active participation. Some of these may test the learner's capacity to find their own solutions before you provide the answer.

Remember to use sight as well as sound; well-chosen visual aids and summary sheets enhance learning. Wherever possible, provide regular practice to consolidate learning, during and at the end of a session. Make sure that there is an opportunity for the learner to incorporate and use new learning in the workplace.

Mentoring

Mentoring can be described as an agreement between an experienced and a less experienced colleague, where the more experienced provides help and support to improve the job performance of the 'mentee' (a horrible word, but better than repeating 'the person who is being mentored').

The learning opportunities in mentoring

Mentoring usually involves working on more fundamental job-related issues, such as management development, career direction or improving relationships and performance. A mentor is often based in another department or even another organization; this should lead to greater objectivity and confidentiality. Mentoring can encompass elements of specific coaching on various skills.

Defining the mentoring contract is a prerequisite if the relationship is to grow and be useful. To create trust and confidence the mentor must be fully aware of what is involved and stick to commitments, particularly those on confidentiality. The mentee must take the time and make the effort to formulate requests for help and make sure that when a meeting or a phone call with the mentor is to take place, the necessary preparation has been made.

Here is a checklist for a draft mentoring contract; it is written from the mentee's viewpoint. This assumes that the mentee is the person who has the most investment in seeking help and they should be encouraged to set up the contract with their mentor. In some cases, though, you as their manager may need to act with them.

1 What type of help do you as the mentee need?
2 What type of help can your prospective mentor offer? Remember you are looking for the best match, although there will be some element of negotiation when you talk the idea over with your chosen mentor.
3 Do you need to supplement the help offered by some coaching on specific skills from another source?
4 How long will the initial period of mentoring run, before you review its effectiveness?
5 How do you want to communicate? For example, will it

be face to face, by phone, e-mail or letter, or a mixture of all of these?
6 What frequency and duration of contact will be feasible for both of you?
7 What ground rules do you need to set? For example, these may include rules on levels of confidentiality and responsibility for decisions made.
8 How will you both review the process of your mentorship? For example, will you set aside ten minutes at the end of a discussion to see what you are both learning about ways of achieving agreed objectives?

Can you mentor your own staff?

In an ideal world we would all have a mentoring relationship with anyone who works with or for us, and good managers undoubtedly encourage their staff to grow and develop through open dialogue. More commonly, though, if you are introducing mentoring as a feature of your department or organization, you are unlikely to be the best mentor for someone who is directly answerable to you. From time to time, within the confidentiality of the mentoring relationship, an employee may need to review how they work with you and this will be best done with someone else who has the necessary independence.

Managers who wish to use mentoring as a means of enabling less experienced staff to grow towards their development potential will therefore need to create networks with other potential mentors.

Project work

In some jobs project work is the main mode of operation, for example in the media industry, in architecture or engineering design. As colleagues work in a small team they get to know each other's professional and personal strengths and weaknesses. There are many other work situations where it is necessary from time to time to set up a project to meet a particular need.

The learning opportunities in project work

If the team is well balanced and effectively managed, its strength is greater than that of the sum of the individual members. Project work has a dynamic of its own. In the early creative stages, needs are defined and quantified and a number of solutions are explored. The project life-cycle, methods, resources and success criteria are mapped out. As the work hits inevitable problems, different skills and qualities come into play. If the project is successful, it concludes with a sense of achievement and euphoria for those who have delivered it. If it has not met all its objectives, there is a period of intense learning which positive management can turn to advantage.

Some people's work experience, however, involves fewer projects. For example, service providers or maintenance and administrative staff are primarily concerned with delivering day by day, week by week, to agreed standards. However, projects do need to be tackled from time to time; for example, there may be a drive to improve service quality to meet a charter, or it may be necessary to introduce a new computing system to handle management or sales information.

No matter how frequently or infrequently your organization or department works on projects, the training and development opportunities they present are considerable. If you always work in this way you will no doubt regularly review through staff appraisal how people can improve and extend their skills. It is perhaps too easy to play safe and always give people the same roles within a project team. Of course some of these roles can only be carried out with appropriate professional training and qualification, but many are more general. There are people skills, such as communication, delegation, motivation and negotiation which your staff can learn more about through structured practice and rotation of responsibilities. There are also project management skills that can only be fully developed and tested if you provide the opportunity for staff to acquire them.

Project teams often do not stop to review the process of working together. Meetings are concerned with monitoring and planning tasks and less frequently with finding better ways to use the diversity of talents in the group or solutions to interpersonal problems that are draining energy and commitment.

The value of process reviews

Consider setting aside time, say half an hour, for a process review during project planning meetings. By 'process review' is meant reflection and discussion on the way the group works together and how it may be improved. In order to avoid the discussion descending into point scoring or conflict, ask the group to agree some ground rules. These might include:

- concentrating first on what can be learnt from successes;
- tackling failure positively as an opportunity to learn, not an excuse to blame or punish;
- being open to feedback, provided it is objective and supported by evidence.

Of course, there are things which happen in work groups which make people's blood pressure rise, and you might hear something like: 'You have landed me in it again! Why can't you get your act together? You're always late – everyone knows what an idle lot you are in your section; someone should sort you out!' This level of aggression may make the speaker feel relieved temporarily, but may cause damage within the group. More to the point, it is unlikely to have the desired effect on the recipient(s).

A project group needs to be able to handle such situations which arise from time to time. Where it is necessary to express disappointment or anger, it should be expressed from the speaker's point of view in terms of how it affected them. For example: 'When your results were two days late, it made me feel very pressured and I had to put up with a lot of flak from Logistics. I felt this was very unfair because it was not my fault. I don't understand why the delay happened. How can we make sure that it does not happen again?'

A process review might run in the following way:

1   Start by taking feedback on things that have gone well and ask people to focus on why they went well. 'What can we learn from the fact that problem X was solved faster than expected?' or 'We have found a new way of handling this part of the process; can we use the same technique anywhere else?'
2   Look at the bottle-necks and problems next and keep the focus on how the team is handling them. Do not slip back into trying to solve them. Work only on improving the way you tackle problems and learn from the process.
3   Ask people to say briefly one thing which they would like to change about the way the team behaves and operates. If some of the answers are a bit negative or sharp, so be it. Don't go on the defensive or let others do so. These feelings are better out than in. Only pick up on them if they are not clear and need brief amplification.
4   Conclude by asking each person to say what extra contribution they are going to make to ensure that the project succeeds.

Work shadowing

Work shadowing will involve you in arranging for one of your staff to work alongside a colleague in your work group or elsewhere, within or outside the organization.

The learning opportunities in work shadowing

The value of this process has been long recognized in work placement when, for example, school pupils spend a week or two in a work environment. It is also the basis for a rudimentary form of training which is often referred to as 'sitting with Nelly'. This described the way in which new members of staff were sat down next to 'Nelly' and left to absorb her practice by example, whether it was good or bad. Work shadowing needs to be better planned than this.

If it is properly structured and managed, it can be a means of giving an employee an opportunity to broaden their view of the type of work that contributes to the success of your business.

Why set up work shadowing?

Some planning and negotiation will be required. Which of the following reasons for setting up a work shadowing programme for an employee fits your situation? Work shadowing may be set up to:

- provide a view of the organization as a whole;
- improve the links and co-operation with an internal or external supplier;
- improve the links and co-operation with an internal or external customer;
- prepare for a possible promotion or move into a new type of work;
- provide an intensive period of coaching;
- achieve a mutual transfer of knowledge or skill.

Can you identify any other reasons in your particular case? If so, make a note of them.

How to set up work shadowing

Discuss the proposal with the member of staff who will shadow. Share with them your reasons. Check that their current work-load will be met by suitable cover from the rest of the work group.

Talk over the proposed shadowing with the other party involved to ensure their commitment and availability. Clarify the role that you want them to play; this will need to be an open and supportive one which will enable the shadow to ask questions and have access to relevant information.

Formulate some learning objectives for the shadowing and agree them with both parties. Have some simple ground rules to cover issues of confidentiality and reference back to you if for any reason the agreed learning objectives are not going to be met.

How to review work shadowing

At the end of the week, or however long the shadowing lasts, make sure that you debrief the shadow to see how far the agreed objectives have been met. You may also find that additional objectives have been achieved and new insights generated. Make sure that there is scope for your member of staff to use this new learning.

Talk through the process with the person to whom your shadow was attached. See what has been learnt and get further feedback on your member of staff.

Summary

The development opportunities described in this chapter are well within the scope of any manager to implement. No doubt you are already using some. If, for example, you are not delegating some of your work, now is certainly the time to start. The point in reviewing these different work-based opportunities is to identify how they can generate learning for your employees and also for yourself. If, for example, you have not so far established an Action Learning set or made little deliberate use of coaching or mentoring, consider starting some pilot exercises with some of your staff now. Next time you need to form a project group or working party to tackle a particular task or issue, make more explicit for everyone the need to learn about how you work best together. There may be other learning opportunities for individuals in the project too; for example, they may have practice in preparing and presenting a project report for the first time.

In the next chapter you will consider what learning opportunities your staff may benefit from outside the workplace.

Reading on

Some of the topics covered in this chapter do not call for further reading; others have been more thoroughly written about. For a very usable general guide to work-based learning, try:

Honey, P. (1994), *101 Ways to Develop Your People Without Really Trying*, Dr Peter Honey, Ardingly House, 10 Linden Avenue, Maidenhead, Berkshire SL8 6HB.

Other helpful books include:

Inglis, S. (1994), *Making the Most of Action Learning*, Aldershot: Gower.
James, R. (1995), *The Techniques of Instruction*, Aldershot: Gower.
MacLennan, N. (1995), *Coaching and Mentoring*, Aldershot: Gower.
Revans, R.W. (1979), *Action Learning*, London: Blond and Briggs.

■ 8

Training and development opportunities outside the workplace

One of the themes of this chapter is that new environments reveal new qualities in employees and release new energy. Another is that a change is as good as a rest. Despite new patterns of employment such as outsourcing and sub-contracting, the great majority of organizations still require people to come to their premises to work. Despite e-mail, teleconferencing and teleworking, face-to-face communications still have many operational and social advantages. The disadvantage of working together in the same space may be the predictability and insularity that this engenders. As one manager commented recently about his overcrowded but air-conditioned workplace as he met me in the lobby during a heat wave, 'This is the only time I enjoy coming here'.

It is not suggested that the activities in this chapter can compensate for inadequate work environments or cure the unpleasant effects of sick buildings or tiring commuting. Indeed, you may be lucky enough to enjoy very good accommodation and facilities. Even so, we all get stuck in certain predictable tracks, and development activities which give you a different perspective from time to time can be invaluable.

The aim of this chapter is to help you to identify a range of off-the-job training and development opportunities and assess their relevance to your work situation. To achieve this you will be asked to:

- *identify the benefits and costs of different types of off-the-job training and development opportunities;*
- *consider what role such opportunities may have in your overall development plan for your staff.*

These are the topics you will be reading more about:

- *away days;*
- *outdoor learning;*
- *community action;*
- *secondments and exchanges;*
- *study visits and exhibitions.*

Away days

Away days are those events where you go as a group to an off-site venue, such as a hotel or residential training centre, with an agreed agenda, to discuss and work on issues that will improve the performance of the group. Away days are often thought of as mainly for managers and mainly concerned with developing a new sense of mission and direction. There are however many other groups and purposes that this sort of event may serve. Here are some examples:

- an induction day for new staff;
- an in-company training day which is deliberately not held on-site, so that people can also enjoy each other's company in a new setting;
- a problem-solving day for a group of staff who are experiencing some difficulty;
- a planning day to enable a work group to concentrate on a task without distractions;
- a team development day.

Although we refer to an away day in the singular you may also consider the advantages of making the event residential over more than one day. Asking people to work together in a new environment for more than one day can be a very powerful catalyst for change, if properly managed.

The benefits of away days

Away days provide the opportunity for people to:

* get to know each other better;
* clarify where individual strengths and weaknesses are;
* improve communications and openness within the group;
* tackle a group task in a concentrated way free from interruption.

Outside help

For many events of this sort you may judge that you need to employ the services of an experienced facilitator/consultant. In larger organizations you may ask an in-house trainer to act in this role for you. Although there is a financial cost, the benefits of using such help should be fully justified, provided that you approach the selection and briefing of the consultant in a thorough and professional way.

It is important to have confidence in your chosen consultant and to allow him or her sufficient time to understand what the aims and objectives of the event are. This may mean paying a fee for them to do this preparatory work thoroughly. It will obviously be an advantage for both of you if the consultant has already successfully worked with you and got to know some of the issues and dynamics that are evident in the group. Agree ground rules with your consultant so that they and you are sure of what is to be covered. A thorough briefing should be given on any issues which may arise. It is unproductive for everyone if you fail to reveal essential information. Your consultant will feel set up on the day and unprepared for any last minute diversions that he or she is forced to take to get behind the presented problem, so that the ones he or she has been briefed on can be addressed.

If real learning is to occur you should have confidence in your consultant and allow them to respond openly and without favour to any issue that may affect you or any members of the group.

Do not rule out the possibility of you and some colleagues

planning and running a day, particularly if it is very task focused and designed to achieve some planning activity. A consultant becomes more important if the emphasis is on the process of the work group, its relationships, its mission and the way it communicates or handles problems. Then the independence and consultancy skills that an outsider can offer may be invaluable.

The costs of away days

As the manager who takes the initiative in setting up the day, you will need to set aside time to plan it so that it achieves defined objectives. There may also be a 'cost' for you and participants to meet in re-thinking attitudes and ways of working as a result of what happens during the day. Indeed, if this is not the case, you may question how successful the event has been. Change requires letting go and finding energy to take up new patterns of work, and this may be a necessary but unsettling cost for you and your work group. Usually, too, there will be decisions and plans made which should be seen to be followed up, so you and nominated colleagues must schedule time to do this after the event.

The cost of a good consultant has already been mentioned. This may fall anywhere between £500 and £1,500, depending on the experience and expertise of the consultant and the importance and complexity of the task you are asking her or him to do.

For participants there may be a problem if the day and the travelling time extend too far beyond normal work hours. Child care and other domestic arrangements may be hard to reorganize, so talk this through with those concerned and allow sufficient notice for alternative arrangements to be made.

There will be travel and delegate costs to meet. It is not essential to choose an expensive hotel; by looking around you may be able to make savings. There is a great variety of venues which put the emphasis on a pleasant environment and healthy food without being punishingly spartan. You will not want to have too long a journey either, particularly for a one-day event. If much is at stake in achieving a successful event you may consider going to look at a new venue before booking it. A number of training venue agencies will find somewhere to suit your specification. For a recent away day event the manager provided transport for her work group by driving them in one of the organization's mini-buses. This provided a cost saving as well as a way of starting the group process from the moment they turned out of the company car park.

Outdoor learning

Outdoor learning uses physical activities as the stimulus for learning about such processes as team building and leadership. Most providers of this type of programme make clear that the level of physical ability needed is no more than 'office fitness'. Outdoor learning can also be used to enhance communication and problem-solving skills. The programme is usually built around a real physical task or journey with stages and targets. The crucial difference between a satisfactory learning experience and 'a bit of a lark' lies in the creative design of the tasks and the quality of facilitation that is offered after each stage in the journey or project.

Much of what has been said about the benefits and costs of away days applies to outdoor learning events; but there are things which outdoor learning can do particularly well.

The benefits of outdoor learning

The event can provide participants with opportunities to learn how to manage valuable resources such as time and the strengths and knowledge of the individual team members. Members should increase their capacity to manage the unpredictable. The creativity of the group is tested, as well as its cohesiveness.

This is all done within the framework of a learning exercise in a stretch of open countryside. The facilitator's role is to press participants to provide a commentary on the process of what has happened or from time to time to offer their own understanding of that process. It can be exacting to engage in the intellectual and emotional task of recognizing how your behaviour has helped or hindered the group. This approach to learning requires expert facilitation as well as the more practical support from qualified staff if such activities as rock climbing or canoeing are involved.

The costs of outdoor learning

There is a much debate about how well learners can transfer insights and awareness gained from the hillside or lake to the office or workplace. Where a work group is able to go through such a process together, there will undoubtedly be gains in team building and bonding that will be hard to achieve in other ways. This does depend, though, on choosing the right provider and on your taking an active involvement as manager before, during and after the event.

Programmes of this sort will not be cheap. They may, for example, involve travel to specialist centres in rugged countryside. You will need to spend time selecting the right programme for your group and budget. You should also consider attending the programme as you should experience or have experienced the process that your staff undergo.

How to find a suitable provider

There are a number of well-established providers. One way of making a choice is to speak to the National Association for Outdoor Education, 12 St Andrews Churchyard, Penrith, Cumbria CA11 7YE; tel: 01768 891065.

Community action

By 'community action' is meant anything from entering a team in the local raft race or half-marathon to seconding a member of staff to work for a charity or community project for a period of time. Some of your staff may be invited to become members of a school or college governing body. An important area for community involvement is through business education partnerships and enterprise programmes for young people.

The benefits of community action as a development opportunity

Let's start with the raft races. What benefits can nearly drowning yourself on a Saturday afternoon offer in terms of staff development?

In some organizations self-revelation is not encouraged. By this is not meant what you look like when you rise like Neptune or Aphrodite from the local lake. The extent to which self-revelation is regarded as permissible depends in part on the culture of your organization. In some organizations you may be valued only for what you can do as a worker, and the fact that you are also an individual with friends, a family and another life outside work may be of little interest to those who manage you. Of course individual workers also have the right to choose how much they wish to share their non-working life with colleagues and managers. However, if people came to work only for the money, life would be simpler, if more socially impoverished. The fact is that what also motivates people to work is the need for a social identity and to be recognized and valued by a peer group and management. Conversely, what is so damaging about sudden redundancy or periods of unemployment is the problem of how to replace the sense of community that work gives, as well as the loss in income.

Back to the raft race for a moment. You will certainly learn more about some of your colleagues as you battle across the pond or lake, as they will about you. Running in a half-marathon with your company name emblazoned on your chest may enhance your sense of identity with your organization as the public see you in a different light. Generating cash for a good cause while having fun must do someone good. Such activities help develop loyalty and commitment. For other members of staff it may be their choice that they form a car rally club or play music together. As a manager concerned about the well-being of the whole person, back these initiatives and, if need be, put at least some of your money where your mouth is.

The costs of community action

If the community action activity takes place in work time, you will need to weigh up the benefits against the cost of lost work. As with many forms of development away from the workplace, you will also need to ensure that the experience that staff gain is talked through so that the learning can be applied and shared at work.

Secondments and exchanges

Working for a period of time in a completely new environment can provide employees with a broader vision. It may also be a means of enabling staff to learn new skills and knowledge as they rise to meet the needs of a new post. You may consider offering a place in your organization for a secondee who can import useful skills, or you may find an opportunity to second one of your employees. You may be able to arrange a simultaneous job swap. Either way, there is a lot to be gained if it is properly planned.

Any ideas involving secondment may sound like an extravagance for smaller organizations, but large companies find that there are clear benefits. So how might the idea be adapted to small companies working on narrow margins? One way may be to consider arranging an exchange, rather than a secondment, so that neither organization is short staffed. There will obviously be a period of induction needed, but provided the exchange is thoroughly discussed and the staff selected with care, this need not be a problem.

The reason secondment happens less than it might is partly because of the demands of running the business on a day-to-day basis. You as the manager may not be looking out for opportunities to second your staff and you may also be reluctant to lose better staff even for a short period of secondment. If you are the one who might provide the secondment position, you may be inhibited by the work involved. You also have to take into account the needs of other staff in your workplace who might see the secondee as a threat or another problem they need to cope with.

The benefits of secondment

The following benefits may result:

- The secondee has the stimulus of a new job without the uncertainties that occur when you really do cut loose and move to a new organization.
- There are (or should be) new types of work experience in the secondment which add to the skills portfolio of the secondee.
- The host organization which provides the secondment position establishes a new relationship and a better understanding with your own.
- You get the training and development you need for your employee, often without having to pay any extra for it.

The costs of secondment

Some costs have already been described in terms of possible disruption to work in your organization. If the secondment runs for a number of months, you will need to consider the individual's need to re-engage with your organization and work group when they return. You may well have to consider finding a different and more challenging position for the secondee so that their new experience and skills are not lost.

What is involved in setting up a secondment?

Although secondment is only temporary, making a secondment should be handled with as much care as when selecting and recruiting a permanent member of staff. Indeed, you may even be in the position of advertising fixed-contract jobs as suitable for a secondment, provided that this does not reduce opportunities for people who are prepared to apply for the post, whether or not they have a job to go back to.

Study visits and exhibitions

Study visits can offer many of the benefits of secondment, although the period away from the job may be shorter and the objectives of the visit more firmly fixed on learning about a particular process or method of working. Visits may be part of a benchmarking exercise where your staff visit another organization not in competition with yours. Such an organization will have been chosen because it has achieved standards of production and service which you aspire to.

You may also receive information from time to time from such sources as the Department of Trade or from your local chamber of commerce about study visits abroad. These will usually be concerned with assessing export possibilities and may be partly sponsored.

Exhibitions can give your staff a stimulus and raise awareness of new developments and products. Many exhibitions include very cost-effective training sessions and seminars which you may be able to buy into on a session-by-session basis.

The benefits of study visits and exhibitions

In both cases the development opportunities are often overlooked. If your staff make a study visit or go to an exhibition without some preparatory discussion and planning, the visit may be wasted. The first step is to weigh up the benefits in terms of what practical contribution the visit will make to the work of the group as well as to the individual. In the case of an exhibition, establish if they are going with a particular brief, such as to:

- collect trade information on a range of new software packages, some new equipment or some new service provider;
- assess what competitors are doing and how well they promote their services;

- look out for trends in the direction the industry is moving;
- be seen and to make contact with suppliers.

If more than one person attends, divide up the 'work' so that the time is used to full advantage.

Expect some report back after the event. Ask a member of staff to make a short presentation at the next work-group meeting.

A study visit has clearly defined objectives and you can expect those who make the visit also to produce a report, which might contain the following headings:

- purpose of visit;
- brief details of locations and contacts;
- main findings of visit, arranged as a series of learning points in priority order;
- action points for your organization;
- assessment of the usefulness of the visit.

The report should not normally be too complicated unless the visit was extensive or designed to gather complex information. One or two pages, which can be circulated and read by those to whom the outcome of the visit is relevant, would be sufficient.

Summary

This chapter should have reminded you that there are important benefits for you and your staff if from time to time development opportunities can be found outside the organization. An away day or days could be the turning-point in building your team. People often refer back to them and to outdoor learning events; they become part of the mythology of the work group.

The other processes described in this chapter achieve an important function in avoiding too much insularity. Keep in touch with the outside world in ways other than through business links with suppliers and customers. Organizations which are not alive to changes in the business and community environment run the risk of foundering. The main message in this chapter is to be open to what can be learned from visits and exchanges and through community action. Do not let off-site experience be wasted; the learning that people gain should be shared and disseminated to colleagues who can use it.

Reading on

Consalvo, C. (1995), *Outdoor Games for Trainers*, Aldershot: Gower. (This is a collection of 63 training games designed for outdoor use. The author is an international expert in outdoor training.)

Bank, J. (1994), *Outdoor Development for Managers*, 2nd edn, Aldershot: Gower. (The author examines the relevance of outdoor learning to the improvement of management performance. The book includes details of 88 outdoor development organizations and a guide to best practice.)

9

Using open learning

Open learning (OL) means a learning system where an individual learns mainly by working through structured materials such as manuals, audio tapes, video or computer programmes. Open learning also requires some tutorial support, either face to face or by phone, fax or e-mail.

It would be interesting to do a small survey among your employees to establish how many people are currently using OL packages and courses, or have done so during the last few years. You may be surprised at how many have enrolled for Open University courses or had access to open learning packages in previous jobs. Open learning is becoming an increasingly common way of meeting training needs and is no longer such a novelty.

The aim of this chapter is to equip you to make an informed decision on whether to use open learning. If you decide to do so, you will be able to plan how best to introduce and support it as part of your training and development strategy. To achieve this you will be asked to:

- *weigh up the benefits and costs of using open learning in your organization;*
- *identify where best to start in using open learning;*
- *choose between buying and making materials;*
- *plan how to induct people to this way of learning;*
- *plan appropriate personal support;*
- *keep track of the progress of individuals and the open learning programme as a whole.*

These are the topics you will be reading about:

- *more about open learning;*

131

- *the benefits of using open learning;*
- *the costs of open learning;*
- *finding appropriate materials;*
- *supporting learners;*
- *how open learning might work in your organization.*

More about open learning

The term open learning, or OL, has been used over the last three decades to describe a process of learning by materials and tutorial support. The Open University (OU) provided, and continues to provide, one very powerful model for the successful use of this way of learning. The OU's version of open learning is frequently referred to as 'distance learning', simply because in most of their courses the learner is necessarily at a distance from Milton Keynes, the OU headquarters. The components which make up open learning – work-books, audio-visual material and tutorials – have been around for some time. Earlier this century there were correspondence colleges and the better of these have survived the revolution in open learning that the OU generated. As well as setting very high standards of materials production and using broadcast channels for distribution, the OU has also developed a technology of education which places the learner, not the teacher, at the centre of the learning process. A key feature designed into all its materials is the learning activity, which encourages active participation rather than passive reading. Through these activities the student has the opportunity to test understanding and develop concepts, skills, techniques, critical awareness and value positions. The university also recognizes that learners need human support and it provides this through its regional tutorial network.

Since the early 1980s there has been a series of initiatives to spread the use of OL into professional and vocational areas. Now more and more organizations are establishing learning centres and CD-ROM based learning packages are more frequently used at work and in the home.

The benefits of using open learning

What can open learning offer you as a manager as you look for options in training and developing your staff? The answer is quite a lot, provided you understand that you need to create the right environment and support for open learners. Some people will always prefer to learn from a tutor with other participants. Others take more naturally to materials-based learning. Some people like the security of a course with known dates and deadlines; others value the flexibility of planning their own schedules and way of working.

The OL method is increasingly used in organizations looking for alternative or supplementary ways of providing training and development. The main advantages are to do with wider choices of learning methods and greater flexibility in use. Sometimes, too, it will be cheaper than more traditional ways.

The 'openness' of OL is usually compared with the 'closed-ness' of more traditional ways of learning and this can be described in terms of the place in which the learning occurs, its pace, its duration, the contents, the methods and the type of assessment that is made (Table 9.1).

Benefits of open learning for the employee

You may, by the way, have felt that 'traditional' learning comes off badly in the comparison shown in Table 9.1. There are some very imaginative and learner-centred courses available in colleges and universities, but often this is because tutors have built greater openness and learner-centredness into their course design.

There is no doubt that the freedom that open learning offers is a positive experience for many people. As you consider Table 9.1, though, you may find yourself thinking that openness could be a bit of a problem for some people. For example, we all tend to work better when we have some sort of deadline to meet. However, an employee who is given the right amount of support and help in planning may find open learning not just the only real option, given work

Table 9.1 COMPARISON OF OPEN AND MORE TRADITIONAL WAYS OF LEARNING

	Open learning	More traditional ways of learning
Place	At home or where the learner chooses	In a college or training centre
Pace	Adaptable depending on other commitments and pressures	To meet the course timetable
Duration	The learner may choose to study over a period of time which suits them	The end of the course, term or year
What to learn about	Some open learning packages offer choices over which aspects of the topic you choose to learn about	Most courses require you to work together from start to finish
How to learn	Learning by yourself, you have the luxury of having several goes at something that you find difficult without feeling foolish	Some courses still rely very heavily on presentations by the teacher or trainer, who may not realize if you do not understand
	OL activities often ask you to reflect on your own experience or go off and do some action research or enquiry	
Type of assessment	The learner may choose whether or not to submit for assessment or use a test within the OL package to self-assess what they have learnt	The assessment methods are laid down by the course provider

and family constraints, but also a positive and novel way of learning.

Benefits of open learning for the manager

To start with the most expedient reasons for using open learning, some managers would see it as a cheap option because they expect people to use the material in their own time. Employees might be invited to borrow a pack and work through it on their own in the evening and at the weekend. Of course, if someone wishes to do this, you would give them every encouragement; but it is not the best way to offer open learning to your staff – not least because less committed staff may compare this way of learning with more conventional courses and think that the organization is taking advantage of staff goodwill.

The other option is to recognize the flexibility that open learning offers and create a learning centre on-site where people can go for an hour or two by arrangement to learn during the working day. Initially, a learning centre can be a space in any training facility that already exists; or you may decide to set aside a quiet space in a separate office. If you are just starting down the open learning route you might even allocate your own office for individuals at times when you know you will not be in. That will have the added advantage that you clear your desk even more regularly! Where there's a will, there's a way; you do not need to go overboard in buying specialized furniture or equipment to get a small learning centre going. Peace and quiet, no phone and a desk and comfortable chair will do for a start. You will, however, have to make it absolutely clear to colleagues that if someone has booked into the learning centre for an agreed period of work, they are effectively off-site and cannot be contacted for that urgent task or message.

The costs of open learning

These depends on a number of factors. If, for example, you are planning to use a package which is based on video or interactive multimedia, you may need to spend between £400 and £750 per set. If, however, you are comparing this with

the cost of sending a number of people away to a course, the package may not seem so expensive.
Initial costs to assess are:

- setting up the process, including searching for appropriate materials, preparing learners and maybe finding someone other than yourself to act as their tutor;
- purchasing or commissioning the materials;
- time out of production, both for the learner and the tutor, plus your time in getting the centre launched;
- paying any assessment fees associated with the course.

Then, as the open learning programme expands and more courses are made available to more learners, you will have to consider the costs of setting up a learning centre. These may include:

- appointing a learning centre administrator to control bookings and keep track of progress of individual learners, assessment records and availability of study space and materials;
- buying audio-visual and multimedia study desks, equipped with computers, video and audio replay;
- expanding the stock of materials to make the learning centre a viable resource.

Then, when your learning centre is a success, you may find that you need to appoint someone to act as the learning manager to develop the quality and momentum of the initiative.

In weighing up these costs against those of more traditional courses, it is worth bearing in mind the following savings that OL offers.

Travel and subsistence

There are no such costs involved in open learning, whereas if you send people on conventional courses travel costs can be as much as the course fee. You also have to allow more time away from work for travel to and from the course.

Reusable materials

If you pay for someone to attend a course, the cost is recoverable only in any benefit that the single learner has derived from attending. Some open learning courses can be used, in part or completely, time and time again. For example, a computer-based package or a learning video should provide a number of years' learning opportunity to many different people. There may be an assessment package that can only be used once, but usually further copies can be bought quite cheaply.

Other costs and benefits are harder to quantify, but where learning centres really catch on and become an essential resource for the organization, a number of corporate benefits follow. These include putting learning more at the centre of the organization, empowering employees and developing managers' skills in helping people learn. Most of these outcomes will not occur if you rely mainly or solely on externally provided courses to meet your training and development needs.

Finding appropriate materials

Materials can either be selected and purchased from open learning publishers or, more rarely, they may be custom made for a particular need within an organization. This is a costly option, but if you work in a large organization with a learning centre, some customized or specially written materials may be produced. Ask your training and development staff.

Most managers only have the choice of using published open learning materials, so how do you track down materials which offer to meet the learning needs that you have identified? There are several ways to start doing this.

You may buy a copy of a directory, such as *The Open Learning Directory* (published annually). You may ask for guidance from your Business Link Information Service. There are commercial providers who act as re-sellers of published open learning material. They will usually have a viewing room and a collection of material which you can look at and assess. Otherwise you could talk to other managers who work in your field to see if they have found any sources which are particularly geared to your needs. Most professional bodies produce training materials, some of which may be in open learning format. Give them a call. Professional journal adverts and reviews will also be useful.

How do you know what material is worth buying?

There is now such a wide choice of training materials on the market that you need a set of clear criteria against which to assess quality. Then, when you have judged the quality of a pack or programme, you need to assess how well it will suit the particular learner you wish to help.

First, how do you judge the quality of the material? Below is a checklist which you can use; you may remember in Chapter 5, 'Choosing training events', you did a similar exercise. Some of the process is the same, in that you are looking for material that has been clearly thought through and which declares openly what it offers to do.

These are the features you would expect to find in a properly produced OL package.

1 *Target users.* The material should make clear who should use the pack.

2 *Level of prior knowledge and experience.* Is it necessary, for example, to have completed an earlier course or to have demonstrated competence by completing some other assessment?

3 *What the package aims to do.* This should be expressed succinctly and unambiguously.

4 *Learning objectives.* Are there any and, if so, do they explain what the user should achieve in working on the material?

5 *Bite-sized chunks.* Is the material divided up into sec-

tions which will help the learner pace their progress in sessions of approximately two hours' duration?

6   A 'How to use' section.   This should give the learner an overview of the material and make suggestions about any other resources that may be needed. It will also suggest options on the sequence and purpose of studying each part.

7   An activity-based approach.   Is the text built around learning activities which require some purposeful response from the learner?

8   Quality of interaction.   This may range from rather undemanding memory tests on what the learner has just read in the pack, to activities which require the learner to tackle more elaborate tasks. These may include analysis, calculation, assessment, formulating and testing hypotheses, reflecting on work experience, and developing and applying new techniques and approaches. The best way to assess this aspect of materials is to sit down with your intending learner and try out a few together – are they stimulating and worth the trouble of doing?

9   Clear signposting.   Is the structure and sequence of use clearly indicated throughout the material?

10 Tutorial support.   What level of support is required? Be wary of packs which claim not to need human support; it would take a very independent learner to work through any significant piece of OL material without needing some sort of help from a colleague, manager or trainer. Later in this chapter you will find some suggestions about the type of help you may offer, or arrange to provide, to any of your staff who learn in this way.

11 Nature and level of assessment.   Does the pack make clear what assessment options are available? Does it contain the necessary materials or do they have to be separately bought?

12 Language.   Is the level and clarity of language appropriate to the declared user group? Is it friendly and unfussy? Does it make things clear and accessible or is it encumbered by unnecessarily complicated terms and expressions?

13 Typographic and graphic design.   Is the layout of material

on the page clear and attractive? If there are illustrations and diagrams, do they add to the meaning of the text and are they clearly presented?

14 *Values.* What assumptions have the producers made about the reader's values? This may cover a wide area from equal opportunities to collaboration and competition. If you cannot subscribe to the values and assumptions that underpin the material, you will need to scrap an otherwise effective pack and look for something which you can support.

Matching materials to learner needs

As you assess the purpose and quality of materials using the questions listed in the previous section, you also need to match the material to the needs of your learners and the environment in which they are working.

To make reasonable judgements about the match you must know your learners. You will have made an assessment of their learning needs using the approaches and techniques outlined in Chapter 4, 'Learning needs and how to analyse them'.

Use the following checklist to see if the learners are likely to respond positively to the materials.

1 *How familiar are your learners with OL study methods?* Is this the first time that they have used OL? If so, how thorough is the material in signposting and explaining how it should be used? How long are the sections? How appropriate is the feedback?

You may consider providing some guided preparation to OL study; there are several booklets which help do this; a very useful one is *How to Win as an Open Learner* by Phil Race.

If they have worked in this way before, it is worth a short conversation to see what they made of it. Ask them what went well and what went less well.

2 *Is the pack going in the same direction as the learner?* Do the aims and objectives coincide with what you as manager

and your learner need to achieve? Talk this over with your learner; give them an opportunity to browse through or view the material. Find an answer to the question, 'If these objectives are met, will this achieve the benefits we are looking for?'

3 *What previous learning does the user need to have completed?* The learners need to be ready for the pack. Does it represent too big or too small a challenge? Is it written in a way that encourages them to read it?

4 *How much tutorial support will learners need?* If you judge that a pack requires significant levels of expert tutorial support to make it work, consider how likely this is to be available to the learners you have in mind. Inadequate support will jeopardize success and discourage learners from working again in this way.

5 *What type of assessment are learners expecting?* If the learner needs some form of accredited qualification as an indication of their achievement, this will influence your choice of package. Some modular courses in supervision and management, for example, will prepare the learner for NVQ assessment. Increasing numbers of courses leading to professional qualifications are now available in an open learning mode.

The person you are helping to learn may not need or want a qualification, however. They may simply want to find out how to do something better or be better informed to do their job.

Involve the learner

In using this checklist you have been encouraged to discuss with the learner or learners the suitability for them of the choice of materials. This will pay off in a number of ways. It shows that you are taking a serious interest in their development. It also enables you to get to know them better and see what makes them tick at work. You will at least have found the best way of helping them learn if the first package you chose does not suit them.

If you are planning on a larger scale and need to provide

learning materials and support for groups of a particular grade or type of staff, you can still choose a small sample and discuss with them the feasibility of the materials for people doing their type of work.

If this whole process sounds too time consuming, given your other management responsibilities, use this as an opportunity to delegate. Assign the planning of your OL initiative as a project for a suitable subordinate; they can then work through the selection process described above. This in turn will give them a development opportunity.

What about multimedia and the Internet?

Reference has been made to text or video materials. There is also a further choice – multimedia – which offers a more flexible and integrated form of learning experience. It brings together, on the computer screen, words, sound, and still and moving pictures, and adds the powerful factor of computing interactivity. As the learner responds to the questions and options on the screen, the computer provides feedback to confirm learning and then opens up further pathways along which the learner can progress. In this way no two learners' experiences of a multimedia package will be quite the same.

The delivery of such packages is currently on either CD-I or CD-ROM. CD-I is a compact disk format that has been mainly used by training providers who have an existing library of their own video productions to use as a visual resource. Although you need a special CD-I player, some providers 'give them away' with the purchase of four or more titles.

CD-ROM (Read Only Memory) is another storage medium which is very versatile in that the disk, which looks like a music CD, can be used on any computer that has a CD player and audio-visual facilities. Given the growth in the number and range of CD-ROM titles, you should find that more and more offices and workplaces have computers with these facilities built into them.

The Internet is already offering exciting opportunities for support and updating of training material via e-mail and other on-line services. As the Internet develops and the speed and quality of global transmission improve, the 'Net' is becoming a powerful means of communicating in all business fields, including training and development. One possible direction for development may be the design of hardware which simply acts as a terminal with a modem, linking the computer to the phone system and thence to the Net. The ever increasing and expensive computing capacity and storage which is being built into PCs may then become less necessary. All the sophistication of systems, applications and courseware will reside in the Net where they can be rapidly updated and improved. The user will simply log into it and use it as and when it is needed.

Another significant development is the use of Intranets, as a form of private Internet linking all PCs within an organization. The possibilities for delivery of company-specific training materials and training support are very exciting.

The rapid growth in multimedia as an OL medium means that the level of interaction between the programme and the learner will become more sophisticated – there will be a closer simulation of the challenges and tasks faced on the job.

However, you will still need to ask yourself and potential learners whether a particular multimedia package is fit for the purpose and whether they are confident they can learn through this medium.

Supporting learners

The materials provide the substance of the learning, but the organizational setting in which they are used must also be supportive and rewarding. Most good OL materials will give guidance on the sort of support that you need to provide for the people who choose to learn in this way in your organization.

What the tutor does can be compared with the job of coaching described in Chapter 7, 'Developing your staff as they work'. Broadly, there are two types of help a tutor can give and these can be described as:

- content related;
- process related.

A tutor should have content skills in the topic which the learner is studying. It would be difficult, for example, to help someone who was learning book-keeping if you yourself had no knowledge of accounting. However, it may not be necessary to have comprehensive knowledge of the topic covered to be able to work through a content problem with a learner. In fact that might be a very helpful experience for both learner and tutor.

Process skills are those which you need as a tutor to understand how the learner is responding and to encourage and help them complete the work. They are the basic development skills you will need whatever the topic being studied.

When to tutor

Induction

The tutor should meet the learner or group of learners before the course gets under way. It is important that the tutor has spent some time looking through the material to become familiar with the way it works and the extent and level of its coverage. The tutor needs to be very clear from the start what the assessment requirements will be and who is to make the assessment.

At the induction stage it is important for tutor and learner to make an agreement about why, when, where and how they will meet. The tutor should also say what they are prepared to offer in terms of tutoring and the time that they have available. This is the time to decide whether to call on anyone else for specialist advice.

Mid-course

Much depends on the duration of use of the materials, but it would be normal to schedule a meeting midway through to see what progress is being made and to solve any problems.

Assessment and conclusion

The tutor will need to arrange assessment if this is part of the package. If, for example, the course is leading to an NVQ, it is for the tutor to discuss with the applicant whether they have completed their portfolio and accumulated sufficient evidence of their competence in all the necessary units and elements for the award. (Do not worry if this sounds a bit technical; you would not be tutoring for an NVQ course without some formal training and preparation by whichever assessment centre you were working with.)

If the course does not lead to a formal assessment for award, it is still important to have a final talk about what has been learnt so that notes can be added to the individual's training and development records. The tutor has a useful opportunity to encourage learners to develop skills of self-assessment, and for learners to acquire skills in receiving and using feedback from a tutor provided it is presented in a clear and constructive way.

Who should tutor

From what you have read above, you have probably built up a picture of the sort of qualities and skills you need to tutor an open learner. It does make a tremendous difference if there is a rapport between the tutor and those they are helping to learn. Open learning tutoring is a very worthwhile development activity for a supervisor or colleague. Spreading tutoring skills throughout the organization will generate other benefits as people become more familiar with managing by helping people learn.

How to tutor

The work does not need to be very time consuming, particularly if the package is not leading to an externally assessed award.

At its simplest, if you have a video-based package on, say,

time management, and a group of staff have expressed an interest in using it, a tutor needs to take the following steps.

1 The tutor sees the video and reads the accompanying materials in advance of the learners.
2 The tutor meets the group to agree the aims and objectives of the learning activity and a schedule and deadline for completion. (The learners then arrange to see the video individually or in groups and work on any related activities in the text at their own pace.)
3 At a second meeting between the tutor and the group, people exchange views and ideas about time management and relate what they have seen in the video to their own work experience. The tutor might suggest that each participant chooses one area of time management to improve over the next three weeks.
4 At a final meeting the tutor might show the video again and ask participants in small groups or pairs to share experiences. The session could conclude by each pair or small group presenting their five best ideas for improving time management.

This is only one short example. You should also take account of the advice given in particular OL packs.

How open learning might work in your organization

Introducing open learning

If you are introducing open learning by yourself, start with a small pilot project. Otherwise you may find that you stimulate more demand than you can handle. You may also consider involving some specialist help, either from within your own training department if you have one or from a local college or independent provider of OL services.

You might have identified a learning need which you cannot meet by sending someone on a course or by arranging some coaching within your department or organization. Talk over with the potential learner the option of using some open learning materials. Follow the materials search and matching processes described earlier in the chapter. Then plan with the learner a schedule and some milestones towards completion of the pack or course. You should also identify someone inside or outside the organization who is qualified to act as a coach or tutor for the learner.

Taking the development step by step, you may decide on the basis of a short pilot that you need to expand the number of courses and packages available so that more people can benefit from this way of learning. At this stage you will be on the brink of setting up a learning centre and this means getting some expert help on the best way to maximize the return on your investment. The more materials you have, the more you will need some form of library management. The more learners you invite to use them, the more tutorial and learner record management you will need. This is, however, the direction in which most national and multi-national companies are moving and it should offer the same development opportunities for your organization as it is doing for theirs.

Summary

This chapter has given you an opportunity to assess the benefits and costs of using open learning as a development method in your organization. The chapter started by defining what is meant by openness in learning and compared it with more traditional ways of learning.

Then you considered how to find open learning materials and how to ensure that, when you do, their quality will meet your needs and expectations. You were given a checklist to help you do this.

Just as with any other form of training, you will need to match the materials to the needs of the learners. You will also have to consider how to introduce what may be for some a novel way of learning.

Learning technology includes multimedia and you were reminded of the potency of the Internet and the Intranet as a means of delivering learning and supporting learners.

Open learning needs the support of people acting as tutors. You were asked to think about who should tutor, and when and how they should do it.
Finally, you were invited to think about ways of introducing open learning into your organization.

Reading on

Open Learning Directory, (annual publication), Oxford: Pergamon. (Contains over 2,000 open learning titles, including computer-based and multimedia material. It will also help you track down providers of OL services.)

Race, P. (updated 1996), *How to Win as an Open Learner*, Coventry: National Council for Educational Technology. (A highly readable and pocketable book intended for distribution to anyone in your work group who is planning to use open learning.)

■ 10

Planning a training event

In this chapter you will first identify situations where it would be appropriate for you to plan and deliver a training session for your own staff.

You will need to build on a firm foundation of training needs assessment, so you may want to refer back to Chapter 4, 'Learning needs and how to analyse them'.

The chapter will then move on to the preparation stage. You will be offered a framework to prepare yourself thoroughly.

The aim of using this chapter is to enable you to plan your own training event. To achieve this you will be asked to:

- *work through four key planning tasks which help ensure that the event is an effective learning experience;*
- *rehearse the cycle of planning, delivering and evaluating an event.*

These are the topics you will be reading more about:

- *to train or not to train?*
- *getting to grips with planning;*
- *preparing to train.*

To train or not to train?

Why might you choose to run your own training event? Here are some possible reasons.

- There is no open course or workshop available which will meet the training needs of your staff.
- The available events are too general to suit your particular needs.
- There are practical problems preventing attendance, for example the course is too expensive, inconveniently timed or too far away.
- You have considered inviting in an external trainer but do not think that this will work.
- You have gained in confidence in your own training skills and feel you are the best person to run the event.

You might choose not to run your own training session if you find that any of the factors listed above do not apply. For example, with a little more enquiry you may find suitable open courses or find trainers who can be briefed to run the event for you; or you may decide that you are too close to your work group to deal objectively with some of the issues which may come up – in this case it would be much more effective to have an external person run it for you.

If you have never tried to train before, you may feel it is a very specialized thing to do. Of course, you need to prepare thoroughly and use some basic skills as you run the event, but this chapter will provide you with all you need to know to get started. Use all the communication skills you have developed as a manager. If you concentrate on the needs of the group and get them involved early, most or all of the stress will go out of it. Then, of course, it is a case of practice making better.

If you are considering doing some of your own training in the near future, think of a particular case which may arise. Make a note under the following headings to summarize why doing it yourself is the best choice for you.

1 What is the training need that you have to meet (for example, introducing a new system of working, improving customer care, setting up a new procedure for processing work)?
2 Which group do you plan to train?
3 Why should you train them?

Having made the choice, what are the next steps you should take to prepare?

'Is my feeling of apprehension unusual?'

No.

First, it is a fact that experienced trainers still go through a period of anxiety and doubt when they sit down to plan a new workshop or course, or prepare to deliver familiar material to a new group. Some level of anxiety is probably good as it will encourage you to put in a lot of effort to make the event as appropriate and effective as possible.

Second, experienced trainers have learnt that although planning and delivery is important, it can become over-elaborate and possibly, during the event, even get in the way of the learning process and the outcomes which will most benefit the learners. Certainly, well-planned presentation is important in most courses, but what really matters is the learning relationship you establish with the group. You should constantly be asking yourself what it is that they are saying they need and what is helping them to learn. In other words, never lose sight of the fact that you cannot learn for other people; you can only make it more likely that they will use the learning opportunities you create for them.

Getting to grips with planning

You have already made some notes above about the training need which you are aiming to meet. This has to be the anchor for any planning that follows. Often at this stage of planning people find it difficult to get over the 'blank sheet of paper' trap and the task of getting to grips with the plan can seem daunting. Where to start? How to be sure that the plan you choose will work?

Think your way through each of these four aspects of your training event.

1   What you want people to know and do when they have finished (*aims and objectives*).

2   What topics and activities they will need to complete (*content*).
3   What learning methods you will help them to use (*methods*).
4   What assessment methods you will use to measure how well objectives have been achieved (*assessment*).

In planning a training event, think how each of these four elements relates and how they may be designed to meet the needs of learners. Some people who start planning events concentrate exclusively on one element – content. For example, if you plan to train people in some topic which you know very well, you may be tempted to design the programme by chopping up the content into a logical sequence and working your way through it. If the course is very much concerned with informing rather than developing skills and reviewing and changing attitudes, you may get away with this approach for a while. However, we can all remember experts who bored us into the ground because they simply delivered the content which they knew inside out, without thinking about the method of delivery or what objectives they were trying to achieve in inflicting the content on us. They almost certainly had no understanding of what we had learnt at the end of it all. If they were in tune with what was going on they may have inferred that something was wrong because half the group were in a day-dream and the rest had left or were becoming fractious. In other words, content by itself is not enough. It has to be:

- the right content for the learning needs of the group;
- content for a purpose – what objectives, outcomes and competences will learners achieve?;
- content which is available to people in ways which satisfy their different learning styles;
- content which is exciting and interesting for this particular group;
- content which can generate learning which is assessable even if that assessment is informal and self-reported (as opposed to formal and external, like a test or an exam).

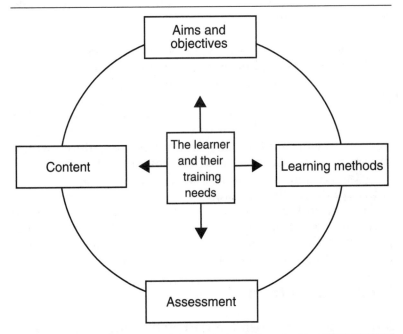

Figure 10.1   RELATIONSHIP OF THE FOUR ELEMENTS
OF TRAINING

The opposite situation might arise where the person preparing to train thinks mainly of the methods and fails to
prepare and structure the content in a meaningful way. For
example, it is no good being convinced that everything can
be done through small-group activities if some of the learning
depends on a clear presentation of a theory or a sequential
demonstration of a process. This trap may lead to the event
being high on togetherness and low on learning outcomes.

The relationship of the four elements is shown in Figure
10.1. There is a direct relationship between each of the four
dimensions of the circle; in changing one you need to see
how it affects the other three.

Consider the example of an initial skills development workshop for PC users; perhaps you have evaluated and become
familiar with a new word processing package and are plan-

ning to introduce it in the office. You decide to spend a few hours making sure that your office staff get up to speed quickly.

So the *aims and objectives* of the event or events will focus on developing skills, but to do this learners will also need to acquire basic knowledge of the software application. You will also have to plan how much *content* to cover and in what order. On the *methods* dimension you might decide whether to demonstrate first, produce worksheets or maybe ask the learners to work individually for a while on a tutorial within the software application. You will have to think about how long the session or sessions should last and what your role is in supporting the learning.

To come full circle to *assessment* you will need to choose ways of measuring the competence of each user by some practical task at the end of the event, or you will not know if the learning objectives have been achieved.

Preparing to train

Most people find it useful to start by thinking about the aims and objectives of the event. You will remember from Chapter 5, 'Choosing training events', that this was one of the aspects of training you would examine in making your choice. At first you may find it difficult to identify good assessable objectives, so let's start there.

Aims and objectives

Knowing what you are aiming to achieve in running a course is essential. It constitutes your aim as trainer.

Break down this aim into objectives, so that you and the participants understand what they should know or be able to do by the end of training. Training is concerned with changing behaviour; in this case, whatever you have already identified through your training needs analysis.

It is good practice to include in your plan for a course a short statement on your aims and the objectives you intend your learners to achieve.

Supposing you were going to run a session on personal safety for a group of reception staff, your aim might be worded like this: 'This course aims to give you a method for identifying risks to your personal safety and plan ways of reducing them.' This is the target that you are setting out to achieve. Then ask yourself, 'What will participants know or be able to do by the end of the course?'

In answering this question you are defining your objectives. They are usually written out in programmes: 'By the end of this programme, you will be able to: (1) ... (2) ... (3) ...', etc.

The more action words, such as 'identify', 'assess' or 'plan', the better. Woolly objectives, like 'Develop a greater understanding of ...', probably mean that the event will be woolly as well. Another advantage of clear objective setting is that you can use the objectives to assess what has been achieved at the end of the event. It is usually unhelpful to have more than four or five objectives for a short training event, as everyone, you included, may lose sight of some of them if there are more.

So, in the case of the personal safety training session, we might decide that the objectives will be written as follows:

By the end of this programme, you will be able to:

1 identify the main hazards to personal safety in your job;
2 assess your personal safety risks according to their severity and frequency;
3 observe and interpret the behaviour of members of the public coming into reception, to assess whether they pose a risk;
4 use a range of techniques to gain control of difficult face-to-face encounters in reception.

Use the following checklist to help you work through the main stages of preparation.

1 Clarify aims and objectives using a learning needs assessment to guide you.
2 Decide on the type and duration of event you will run;

for example, a small coaching session, a half-day or one-day workshop.

3 Clarify for yourself what role you as the trainer will adopt – sole tutor, co-tutor with a colleague, instructor, facilitator.

4 Choose and sequence the content. Avoid overloading the programme.

5 Select appropriate training methods (in the next chapter you will find a compendium of methods with examples showing how and when to use them).

6 Choose what method you will use to assess how well learning objectives have been achieved.

7 Prepare handouts and visuals. Be selective. Too much material will be unhelpful. Make the visuals big enough to read and keep them simple.

8 Produce a trainer's plan in which to note what you are going to cover in each section and how you plan to run it. This acts as your prompt and guide.

9 Plan domestic arrangements. Check fire alarm and exit arrangements, loos, smoking regulations, tea and coffee, and food. There is a further note on preparing the physical training environment in the next chapter.

10 Decide on the best way to evaluate the event – an evaluation form, verbal feedback or both? Again you can find some further guidance on evaluation in the next chapter.

Summary

Having read this chapter you should have the basic tools to hand for planning your own training event. First, you considered under what circumstances you might decide to run a training event for your staff. You have learnt about the four aspects of planning – aims and objectives, content, method and assessment. You then worked through a checklist to help prepare for the session. Training methods and ways of evaluating sessions will be described in the next chapter.

You may well find that training events for your own staff can be run fairly informally and do not necessarily have to be very long. The planning material you have covered in this chapter could help you prepare a one-hour session as part of a team or work-group meeting. Try it; it is the only way to learn. You may also choose to involve one or two of your group to work with you. There are some further suggestions on doing this at the end of the next chapter.

Reading on

Prior, J. (ed.) (1994), *Gower Handbook of Training and Development*, 2nd edn, Aldershot: Gower. (A widely read 'standard'. Includes chapters on cultural diversity, learning styles and choosing resources. Forty-nine experienced training professionals have contributed to this book.)

■ 11

Delivering a training event

In the previous chapter you laid the groundwork for running your own training session. We now turn to what happens in the session and consider how you can keep control of yourself and your training plan, not to mention the participants' attention. An important clue to successful operation lies in adopting a participative approach. Get your learners working with you; use their ideas and suggestions. This gives you a break from being the presenter and the ultimate expert. You will find some useful guidance on how to deliver the event with confidence.

To conclude, you need to collect feedback and other evidence to see how well the learning needs were met during the event.

The aim of this chapter is to equip you to deliver and evaluate your own training event. To achieve this you will be asked to:

- *review a range of training methods and identify suitable applications for them;*
- *plan the effective use of audio-visual resources;*
- *prepare the room and the domestic facilities;*
- *plan how to evaluate the session when it is complete.*

These are the topics you will be reading more about:

- *what is meant by the participative approach?;*
- *a compendium of training methods;*
- *using audio-visual resources;*
- *looking after the domestic arrangements;*
- *delivering your training session;*
- *evaluating what has been achieved and what to do differently next time;*
- *getting your work group to run a training event.*

Although you need to be able to present information to groups,
much of the time you will be encouraging participation, getting
people to work individually and in small groups on solving problems
by using the ideas and information you provide.

What is meant by the participative approach?

Participants should be encouraged very early on in the
session to share ideas and opinions in response to a clear
framework of questions and activities on the theme of the
training session. Within such an event it is possible to include
short presentations by you or by a sub-group. Other resources
such as videos may also be used as a stimulus or trigger to
discussions. Any detailed factual information that the group
needs can be given out as handouts. If there will not be
sufficient time for reading during the session, the material
can be circulated beforehand or as items to take away.

The way trainers deliver a course is very much a result of
the chemistry between them and the group. So be flexible
and be prepared to read the signs in the group. If they need
more time on one activity you may decide to cover the next
topic briefly.

However, there are certain main ways in which trainers
try to encourage group participation and some of these are
described in the section which follows. You will no doubt
have your own to add to the list.

A compendium of training methods

In this section you will find brief descriptions of some of the
commonest types of participative training activity.

Brainstorming

Brainstorming is a method of generating ideas in a group.
Normal rules of conversation often seem to prevent the flow
of new ideas within a group. The rules of brainstorming
avoid these problems.

1 One person acts as a scribe to record ideas on a card, flip-
   chart or board.
2 Group members may offer ideas but may not justify or
   explain them, or withdraw them after second thoughts.
3 Ideas may not be criticized or clarification sought, and no
   discussion of any kind is permitted.
4 Any analysis and discussion starts only when all ideas
   have been verbalized and recorded. At this point look for
   what is feasible and interesting in all items, then draw
   up a list of those suggestions that are worth developing
   further.

Brainstorming releases the creation of ideas from exposure
to instant criticism and dismissal. It is very useful at the start
of a session as a way of harnessing the inventiveness of the
whole group. It can also be used to get out of dead ends as
a problem-solving activity.

Example

A brainstorm could be based on the question, 'What would
make our working lives less stressful?' Encourage people to
let their imaginations roam freely. Such ideas as 'not coming
to work', 'installing a jacuzzi in the office', can be seen in
later discussion to contain some insights which are worth
developing. How else did such ideas as flexi-time, teleworking and improved staff welfare facilities come to be
developed and accepted?

Buzz groups

In this method a large group is divided into smaller groups
for a short period to give people more opportunities to
exchange views. It also gives participants a chance to re-
engage if they have been passive for some time. It creates
more ideas and opinions and can generally raise the energy
and motivation levels. The 'buzz' which nearly always
follows such a restructure gives rise to the name for this
method.

Use buzz groups when the group is stuck for ideas, if some learners are not confident enough to speak out or are being silenced by more vocal members of the group. Use them also if a decision has to be made and people need to consult in smaller groups before making up their minds, or if there appears to be collusive agreement and the group lacks the diversity of different views and opinions.

You will need to manage the breaking down into smaller groups and set the time boundaries. Make sure everyone knows what the buzz groups should be tackling and ask them to nominate a spokesperson who can report back briefly, supported by some headings on a flip-chart. (See 'Plenaries' below).

Example

During a session on improving customer care, buzz groups could address the question, 'What three things would most improve our current level of customer care?'

Instruction and demonstration

If you are teaching your group a technique or process which is new to them you will need to communicate it very clearly and demonstrate how to do it. You will also encourage them to ask questions and then practise the process. This will help you measure how well they are understanding and let you know when they have achieved the agreed learning objectives. You will recall that there is a section on instruction and demonstration in Chapter 7, 'Developing your staff as they work'. In it there is a checklist on how to do this. It was included there because you often need to give a demonstration in the workplace. However, this approach to instruction and demonstration is just as applicable if you plan to run a group training event.

Checking expectations

Participants may wonder at the start of a training session what they will be asked to do, and whether the course will prove useful. An exercise which involves movement, imagination, sharing and fun could begin the process of building an environment conducive to learning. It will also act as an ice-breaker.

Examples

People may be invited to write on one side of a postcard, in not more than one line, what they most hope to get out of the session, and on the other side what they want to avoid happening during the session. They place the cards anonymously in a heap, then draw out another card. Everyone in turn reads out the two sides of the card they have chosen. A very brief discussion can be run to acknowledge people's hopes and fears. It is probably best if this does not last for more than ten minutes. An exercise like this is designed to engage the group members by focusing on the job in hand.

Another example might be to ask people as a simple ice-breaker to tell each other in pairs what has been the best thing to happen to them during the last twenty-four hours. This will release a lot of energy and laughter and ease the way into the session.

Continua

A continuum is a method whereby a group of learners are asked to range themselves along a continuum, or an imaginary line on the floor, which represents an issue or a situation. At one end is a particular view of the issue, at the other is the opposite view. The two ends should represent *equally valid* views on the issue.

It can be a very useful way of demonstrating a wide range of different views or positions within a group, and the fact that learners have to place themselves physically somewhere on the continuum means they will consider their views very carefully. Suggest that they discuss with their neighbours why they have chosen their position on the line.

Examples

The continuum can be used in a wide variety of situations and is a highly appropriate method of examining in detail the nature of any conflicts present within a group. The continuum participants have to define what their different views are; in fact they are openly encouraged to do so. This reduces the personal dimension of conflicts within a group and puts them more into a framework of different beliefs or values.

Another example might be to ask people to arrange themselves along a continuum line to reveal factual information which may not be known to all participants, such as the length of time they have worked for the organization.

A third example might be to invite participants to range themselves along a continuum where one end represents the view that the organization is too slow to respond to change and the other that the organization is getting lost in sea of change.

As the organizer of a continuum, you will need to:

* ensure that the ends of the continuum represent valid views;
* establish certain ground rules – it is not about guessing which is the 'right' end;
* encourage the positive view of differences;
* manage the feedback so that you can use the self-revelations people make as a springboard for some planning and development.

Plenaries

This is a method of bringing a group back together after they have worked in small groups or individual and sub-group assignments. They tend to occur at the end of an important session and they can offer significant learning opportunities.

They are built round a series of short reports from spokes-people who present sub-group findings or plans.

Plenaries need to be controlled, as they can either become very rushed and ineffective, or get slower and slower. Set strict time limits for each spokesperson's exchange and work out beforehand how long you need to set aside for this part of the session.

It may not always be necessary to use a plenary. If people want to discuss matters with each other this could be accomplished on a more informal level.

As the organizer you will have to be able to manage feed-back, and be prepared to ask the contributor for further clarification on points; but avoid 'smartening up' or capping their presentation yourself.

Role-play

Learners play a role and in so doing practise and develop skills of communication, observation, listening and giving and receiving feedback. Role-plays are used to try to get 'under the skin' of other people by setting up situations where you can experience simulated interactions of the kind you encounter in your job. This can lead to a better appreciation of how you behave and why other people feel and behave the way they do. Role-play offers a challenging way of developing skills in giving and receiving interpersonal feedback.

It should be said that some people have a resistance to the very idea of role-play, so you should prepare the ground carefully.

There are four stages to any role-play:

1 briefing;
2 running the role-play;
3 de-briefing (getting out of the role);
4 processing – discussing in some detail the role-play itself and the learning points.

Most role-plays need time to get off the ground; they may

take half an hour or maybe much more. You may have a particular training need or problem that could be best addressed by this training technique. Remember that a role-play which runs only for ten minutes often needs a half an hour's discussion during which all the participants have the opportunity to talk through what happened.

If you are organizing a role-play situation, make sure you:

- explain roles, situation and structure clearly;
- prevent reluctant participants from feeling threatened; (they can be given a role as an observer or recorder);
- assist the group to allocate roles and ensure that all necessary equipment is available;
- keep a close check on time limits;
- manage feedback.

Example

In preparation for a stressful encounter, each participant might play out a role as aggressor or respondent in a particular setting.

Small-group work

Within a training session a small group would usually have four or five members. Small groups work on tasks identified in the whole group and may be working in parallel or on different parts of the same task. They choose their own way of working and their own chair and spokesperson to report on the outcomes of the task.

Small-group work can be used in many situations; for example, whenever participants need to exchange experiences, make decisions or tackle problem-solving tasks.

Some management is necessary to make the use of small-group work effective. You should ensure that:

- all the small groups know and understand the task before the group divides up;

- you are available for further clarification while the task is in process;
- the feedback from the small groups is properly managed and ground rules established so that each group knows how long their presentation will last;
- decisions are taken on how to handle inter-group questions and comment.

Example

You might divide into small groups and ask people to formulate an action plan for raising staff awareness of learning opportunities in the workplace. One group might look at how to gather and use information on training needs in a more systematic way. A second might identify situations where coaching could be offered by staff. A third group might propose a system for introducing mentoring. Another might review current training provision and suggest alternative ways of delivering training.

Snowballs

A snowball is a method of discussing and developing ideas by changing group size from pairs to the whole group in progressive steps.

A topic or a question is set for initial discussion between pairs. They are then asked to work with another pair to summarize the key points of both pairs' discussions. The new groups of four are asked to exchange key points with another foursome, which usually requires them to choose a spokesperson. The session is rounded off with two larger groups presenting their findings to each other.

Snowballs are particularly useful with new groups as they allow everyone in the group to express an opinion in a safe setting. People can relate to and compare with others gradually in the broadening spread of the group. It is a good method of helping a group to warm up and could be a useful corrective to a situation where a minority has dominated a less structured general discussion.

If you are organizing this type of activity, keep a strict eye on timing and instruct the groups to converge at intervals of five to ten minutes. It is also important not to overdo this type of activity.

Example

Set the task of drawing up a checklist of ways to improve productivity in a particular part of the plant by reducing waste.

Using audio-visual resources

If you are booking a training venue outside your organization, ask what is available. What audio-visual resources do you have access to? Most venues will have the following items:

- chalkboards or whiteboards;
- a flip-chart, or cheap paper that could be made into a flip-chart;
- an overhead projector;
- a video.

If you plan to run regular in-house training sessions think about investing in some of these items, probably in the order they are listed above.

Using whiteboards

A board is used to list key points for the group, to show something graphic such as a plan or diagram or to record ideas and information from the group.

The whiteboard is an alternative to the chalk variety, but you do need to remember the following points.

1 Make sure the board is clean before you start; have the cleaning cloth available.

2 Have the right marker pens and check they will not run

out. One important point – they should to be *water soluble*. Avoid spirit-based pens, or you'll need a solvent cleaner to clean the board. You will also be extremely unpopular with anyone who wants to use the room the following day!

3 Write clearly and check that everyone can read what you are writing.
4 Don't forget to address the group, not the board.
5 Write down only key issues and do not expect people to be able to take in vast quantities of writing at one time. Wherever sensible, wipe the board when you've finished with something before going on to the next item.
6 Make sure that people can see; sometimes light reflects off the board.

Whiteboards are good for such exercises as brainstorming, where you can write up a lot of ideas quickly.

Flip-charts

A flip-chart has the advantage that once written on, the sheets can be torn off and displayed around the room, using Blutack or masking tape. These can be kept for future reference, or used in the next training exercise. Flip-charts are, however, expensive and may not be available at all premises.

Remember that the same basic requirements of clear handwriting and clear concise notes apply as for writing on boards.

Videos

Remember the following points when showing a video:

1 Make sure you know how to use the machine before the presentation.
2 Have a very clear idea of your aims in showing the video and what you hope the group will achieve by seeing it.
3 Offer the group a 'viewing framework' by telling them

what to look out for in the video and to note down points they want to discuss afterwards.

4   Videos require an introduction, and you will need the time for a feedback session after the video to discuss the content.

5   Do not show the video straight through, unless it is very short. Consider convenient stopping places for discussion to achieve the maximum learning benefit for the group. Using video as a trigger for discussion is a powerful use of the medium.

The overhead projector

The overhead projector (OHP) is an effective and convenient way of displaying information and emphasizing points. If you have access to one, it has an important advantage over boards and flip-charts in that, in using it, you need never turn your back on an audience.

You can prepare OHP transparencies beforehand using colour and design. You can turn laser-printed paper into acetates on a copier, provided you use the correct copier acetate. (The type you write on will melt in the copier and cause damage.)

Remember the following points each time you use the OHP.

1   Set it up before you start and make sure it is in good working order and the lenses are clean.

2   The screen is in the correct position for everyone to see and the image is sharply focused.

3   You do not stand in the way of the screen.

In preparing the transparencies avoid putting too much information on each sheet. Letters should normally be at least a half an inch high to be easily readable.

Another exciting option for presentation via an OHP is to link it to a laptop computer. This involves using an LCD display which sits on the table of the OHP and displays exactly what you have prepared on the computer. With suitable presentation software, your scope for producing animated full-colour presentations is considerable.

Handouts

Participants usually expect handouts, but ask yourself why and how you are using them.
Use handouts if they:

- can summarize essential concepts and act as an aide-memoire;
- will save laborious copying down of information by participants;
- provide information necessary to the completion of some workshop activity.

Do not use handouts in the mistaken belief that everything displayed on the OHP or a flip-chart has to be put into people's hands. Use them sparingly and consider preparing them as incomplete or 'gapped' handouts. Then you can involve your learners in completing tasks, doing calculations or recording learning points on their handouts. Suggest to them that they see the handouts as their own learning guide which they can customize and modify as the course or workshop progresses. If you do this there is a chance that the handouts will be referred to again after the event. Even so, keep the volume of the material to an absolute minimum. People meet together to interact, to think and respond, not to read and write.

Looking after the domestic arrangements

Your objective in preparing the training room is to allow everyone to be engaged in what is going on and to be free from distractions. If you want people to communicate with each other, it is important to remember that people do so by looking and being seen, as well as by talking. The seating layout will have a direct bearing on this.
A good room layout is to arrange the chairs in a horseshoe

shape or a circle. This ensures maximum visual contact. It also breaks down the invisible barrier between them and you, the organizer and facilitator of the event. You will be familiar with the way some presenters start sessions by saying 'Please move forward and fill up the front seats'. It is unlikely that in your training session you will have so large a group that you need to seat people in rows. In fact, avoid rows of seating at all costs. If learners will be working on paper-based activities, consider providing them with clipboards so that they can make notes as they sit. If they need to spread out a number of papers to work on, you may choose what is sometimes described as 'cabaret' layout; that is, a series of small tables with four or five seats, dotted round the available space. The best arrangement is to have exactly the right number of chairs for the group, so that empty chairs do not constantly make you aware of absent friends during the session. If someone does not turn up, remove their empty seat at the first opportunity.

You may also need access to smaller areas for discussion and short assignments in syndicates of three to five people. If this is the case, set up some separate areas with tables and chairs for this purpose.

In your general preparations, plan some refreshments for tea or coffee breaks. If people have travelled to the event, a welcoming cup of tea or coffee and a biscuit help set a positive expectation for the day. You might decide to place some bottles of mineral water in the room. Hotel venues tend to do this and sometimes provide mints for the obsessive sweet eaters. You might consider having some fruit as an alternative; it need not cost too much and is very popular.

If your budget can run to it, provide lunch. The thing to be wary of in offering lunch is the impact that an over-elaborate binge at the carvery may have on your timetable and people's capacity to stay awake in the afternoon. Something lighter in the form of a buffet makes more sense. People work better in training sessions if they feel comfortable but remain alert.

Delivering your training session

Use the following checklist to help you prepare for the actual delivery of the training session.

1 Share expectations and objectives.
2 Discuss ground rules.
3 Ensure that participants understand that the main responsibility for learning always remains with them.
4 Follow your trainer plan, but check that it is working. (If it is not, don't panic; discuss other options which you have thought through beforehand.)
5 Vary your methods.
6 Divide up the session into manageable parts.
7 Use different senses. Show material as well as talk.
8 Divide the participants into different-sized groups.
9 Re-cap and consolidate.
10 Gather feedback and evaluation.

Evaluating what has been achieved and what to do differently next time

All the work activities that you manage should be evaluated and training is no exception. There are two main focuses to the evaluation. You need to know from the participants:

1 what learning has been achieved;
2 how they felt about the process and the event as a whole.

The extent to which you can actually assess what learning has been achieved depends on the type of learning objectives which were set for the event. If, for example, you were running a presentation workshop, you might include an individual or group presentation as the final exercise of the event. The group could have done some useful preparatory work in drawing up a set of criteria for verbal presentations. It would then be possible to provide some 'formative' assessment to each presenter. (By 'formative' is meant assessment feedback which the recipient can use to 'form' or develop their performance.) At the same time you as the tutor will have some tangible measure of how well the learning objectives of the session have been met.

In other cases, though, such as time management or delegation workshops, you are less likely to be able to gather hard assessment information and you are more likely to be evaluating the second area – how people felt about the process and the event as a whole. The significant difference here is that you are relying on people's capacity to self-assess and to be objective in what they disclose.

The most usual way of evaluating people's reaction is to circulate a short questionnaire at the end of the event. There are many different designs for such questionnaires and you will probably need to use a basic set of questions but to tailor them to fit the objectives, content and methods of your particular event.

Look through the sample form (Figure 11.1) and see how you might adapt it.

Workshop evaluation

Workshop title ....   *Venue*
....   *Date   /   /9*

To help us evaluate this event, please answer the following questions by putting a ring round the appropriate answer.

1 Before the workshop
Do you feel you were given sufficient information
about the event before it began?   *Yes/no*
If no, note briefly what else you needed to know:

2 To what extent did the workshop meet its aim and objectives?
1 not at all   2 to a very limited extent   3 to some extent
4 to a large extent   5 completely

3 How about the content of the workshop?
Was it:
1 too little?   2 sufficient?   3 too much?
1 mainly familiar to me   2 partly familiar, partly new   3 mainly new
1 not relevant to my work   2 relevant   3 very relevant

4 Did the working methods used in the event encourage you to take part?   *Yes/no*
If no, what would you have preferred?

5 Was there sufficient opportunity for you to learn from other participants?   *Yes/no*

6 Any comments about the venue, facilities or refreshments?

7 After the workshop
How useful do you expect the course to be for you back at your workplace? (please tick)
1 not at all   2 of limited use   3 useful   4 very useful
5 very useful indeed

8 What feedback, if any, would you like to give the trainer(s) who ran the event?

9 What feedback, if any, would you like to give your organization as a result of your attending this event?

Please add your name if you wish ....
Department or section ....

Many thanks for your help in ensuring that we continue to offer effective learning opportunities.

Figure 11.1   WORKSHOP EVALUATION FORM

Other forms of evaluation

You may feel that you know your work group too well to give them forms to fill in. Another option would be to ask them to reflect for a moment on what has been most useful for them and what they would have preferred to be different. Then do a round robin where each in turn briefly gives two short statements.

If you think that this will not elicit the information you need, you can suggest that everyone writes their two statements, anonymously, on a card. Ask them to fold the card to hide the writing. All the cards should then be put into a heap in the middle of the circle. Invite people to take one card out, not their own, and read it to the group.

Coming back finally to the question 'What learning has been achieved?', the real measure of the usefulness of any training event is to be found in the improved performance of individuals and the group. As a manager who runs training events, you are uniquely placed to collect evidence on improvements. As you may know, assessment for National Vocational Qualifications (NVQs) is largely based on observation and evidence derived from the workplace. If there is no observable or measurable improvement in competence, you might as well save time, effort and resources by scrapping training. As you manage your work group on a day-to-day basis, you can carry out the most useful form of evaluation of all, recording, discussing and acknowledging improved performance as it occurs.

You can read more on this in the next chapter.

Getting your work group to run a training event

The chapter concludes with some suggestions for handing over some of the responsibility for training and development to the group itself.

To improve the pay-offs of training events you may try an alternative approach to the design of learning programmes. It will require your employees to share with you an increasing responsibility for learning outcomes. You may also consider reducing the amount of time spent in the training room and increasing the amount of work-based practice.

Example

This example is based on improving customer care, although it could be improved communications or a particular development topic of importance to your work group.

In a short introductory session the group can review what objectives it wants to achieve with regard to customer care. You may use some existing resource such as a training video or multimedia package to provide input. You could also ask one or two of your staff members to prepare some handouts and make a short presentation on improving customer care in your organization.

The main purpose of this session will be to prepare participants to complete work-based learning activities, as and when appropriate situations in the workplace arise. If you are aiming to improve customer care in the reception area, you might agree that staff will focus on the following aspects over a two-week period:

- making customers feel welcome on arrival;
- eliciting accurate information about customer needs and questions;
- providing relevant and usable information;
- giving clear directions for further action and help.

The group might work on developing a rating scale for each of these stages of customer enquiry handling. In pairs they can agree to evaluate each other in the workplace for each stage at some point during a specified period of time.

The outcome of these work-based activities will be noted. Any notes and records made by participants will be brought back to a second learning session where they can be analysed and used to structure and consolidate learning.

The advantages of working in this way include:

- pooling and using the wisdom and experience of the group;
- increasing the group's capacity to solve its own problems and value its own learning;
- gaining the commitment of the manager and staff to a common learning process;
- shifting the focus of learning from the workshop to the workplace.

As a manager your role is to share in and help steer this learning process. The more that you can encourage staff to take responsibility for learning outcomes, the better.

Summary

In this chapter you have learnt about the basic techniques and methods that trainers use to ensure participation and involvement. A range of training methods was described and examples of their application were given. You were then reminded about the effective use of audio-visual resources and there was some guidance on sorting out the domestic arrangements.

In the actual delivery you should be flexible and focus on the particular learning needs of the group. You need to establish what has been achieved and evaluate the process of the event. You were given a sample evaluation form which can be adapted to suit your situation.

It may be that from time to time you negotiate with a manager in a separate part of the organization to provide some training for their staff in exchange for some similar help from them. This may take away some of the initial self-consciousness of switching roles from manager to trainer with your own staff.

Finally, you read about ways of involving members of your work group in planning and running a training event with you. This may reduce the sense of training being too far removed from the day-to-day experience of doing the job.

Reading on

Moss, G. (1991), *The Trainer Desk Reference*, London: Kogan Page. (This short and very practical guide starts with a summary of learning theory and then follows through the process of planning and delivering a training session.)

■ 12

Assessing learning outcomes

By making self-assessments and receiving supportive feedback from others, learners acquire an increasing awareness of what they now know or can now do. You too as their manager will want to know that the care and effort that you have put into supporting and encouraging your staff have improved their performance. In thinking about the topic of assessment, you are coming full circle in a learning process which began with the definition of learning needs, the setting of objectives and the creation of development programmes which were designed to meet those needs.

Assessing outcomes and agreeing new goals can be part of the regular pattern of appraisal interviews, but there are good and bad ways of giving and receiving feedback. We touched on this briefly in Chapter 2, 'Helping people learn at work'.

This chapter returns to this theme and provides guidance on how to give good-quality assessment feedback, whether it is in the context of an appraisal or more informally on a day-to-day basis.

The aim of this chapter is to help you to identify different ways of assessing learning outcomes and, in particular, to think about the productive use of staff appraisal as a performance development tool. To achieve this you will be asked to:

- *match assessment methods to particular types of learning;*
- *identify ways of giving effective feedback to staff;*
- *use staff appraisal as an opportunity to review current learning objectives and plan future ones;*
- *assess the use of peer and upward appraisal;*
- *consider ways of recording personal development plans.*

These are the topics you will be reading more about:

- *when and how to assess learning outcomes;*
- *how far learning objectives have been achieved;*
- *giving feedback;*
- *using staff appraisal to improve learning;*
- *using peer and upward appraisal to improve learning.*

When and how to assess learning outcomes

In Chapter 10, 'Planning a training event', you considered ways of collecting assessment information at the end of training sessions run by you or others. Obtaining feedback on the way the event has gone is essential, and included in this information may be some general indication of the type and quality of learning that has occurred. However, as was noted earlier, any responses you collect at the end of events are very much conditioned by the social dynamic of respondents being together for the course or workshop. If participants enjoyed themselves in a pleasant environment, it will inevitably be reflected in the evaluation they give the event. There is nothing wrong with that, provided that was not the only outcome. Indeed, events where the physical comfort of participants is ignored are unlikely to generate much learning.

However, we should also attempt to measure performance improvements and identify which learning objectives have been achieved. This requires you to look at what happens to participants in the workplace after the event. In focusing on this you, as a manager, are in a stronger position than most trainers to learn about the effectiveness of whatever training and development programme you have run or caused to be run by others. You will also be in the mainstream of thinking about assessment. Indeed, an important consequence of the introduction of the National Vocational Qualifications system is that the focus of assessment is fixed on work-based competence. The main task is to assess how well people can do the job. How well do they meet agreed standards? Does their work match up to defined performance criteria?

When should you assess? The sooner the better. It will be easier for you as a manager to assess how a member of your staff has done on an assignment while all the evidence is live and accessible. You will be looking for performance outcomes – did they achieve the targets you had agreed? If, however, you have also identified learning objectives which are a natural spin-off from doing the job, you will want to assess how well they have been met too. You might, for example, discuss what new skills the employee has acquired or any new areas of knowledge they have developed as a result of doing the job.

If you are working closely together on a project, or you have delegated a task and have followed it through at agreed intervals, you can make some form of continuous assessment as the job unfolds. If you are a bit further removed you will want to gather evidence from a number of sources. One important source is self-assessment; ask the person concerned for their views on their progress. Look at the results. Talk to any internal or external customers who may have a view on the quality of the service or products provided.

How far have learning objectives been achieved?

In our basic model of the training process in the previous chapter, assessment was shown opposite aims and objectives. They are directly related and that is why it is worth spending some time trying to define clear and meaningful aims and objectives for a learning activity. If you do not know what objectives may be achieved, it is very hard to know how to assess learning outcomes.

Consider the example of the driving test. The aim of a driving instructor is to prepare someone who has not so far passed, to do so. The objectives that they need to achieve are broadly of two types – to enable the learner to:

1 demonstrate practical skills in driving and manoeuvring the vehicle through a series of prescribed test situations;
2 give correct answers to a series of questions based on knowledge on the Highway Code and accepted good practice in driving.

The standard in meeting these two objectives is laid down by the Driving Test Agency and assessed by the agency's examiners.

The way to assess the attainment of these two objectives is completely different. You can only test the first objective on the road, observing the performance of the candidate. You could test the second verbally through a series of pre-defined questions, either on paper as a multiple-choice test or on a computer as an interactive test.

Satisfactory performance in this second type of test would be no guarantee of the learner's competence to drive. It would also be tedious and distracting to try to test all the knowledge questions during the on-the-road part of the test.

In thinking about assessing the learning outcomes of any training event you arrange for your members of staff, you have to make similar choices. Wherever possible, look for opportunities to assess performance in the real working situation. You will not often need to be as formal in the way you assess as, say, a driving test examiner or an academic examiner. Remember that the point of assessing is not only to measure performance but also to encourage further learning and the growth of confidence. So how would you do this?

An example might be that you have arranged for someone to go for training in maintaining and recalibrating a piece of essential equipment. They should have been given some certification by the course providers that they can now do so to an acknowledged standard of accuracy. In such circumstances all you may need to do is to spend some time with them when they do the calibration. You might say, 'Show me how they taught you to do it' or ask them if you can sit in on the job to remind yourself of the method. You can also gauge how confident they seem in doing the task. This may lead to an opportunity to ask whether they have any uncertainties or need to work with a qualified colleague for a few times to consolidate their new knowledge and skills.

This assumes that you yourself are competent in the process and can confidently distinguish between acceptable and unacceptable levels of performance. If you are not, and you can't, involve someone who can. The cost of inaccuracy could be quite high. Assuming the result of your informal assessment confirms that of the course providers, do not forget to give positive feedback to the employee – 'That's great; you can obviously do this well. It will be very useful to have another qualified person available.'

Another example might be following up the outcomes of a time management course. The employee concerned will have discussed beforehand with you their need to improve and you will have nominated them for a particular course, so you have that as the basis for assessing what has been learnt. If the event has worked for them, they should have identified some action points which they are going to work on. Perhaps they have decided to work on controlling interruptions or protecting their optimum time each day for getting important assignments done. They may also have chosen a new way to organize their dairy or control the paper that flows across their desk. Simply asking what the learner got from the course will help focus their minds on learning outcomes as well as showing them that you attach importance to getting some benefit for the organization from the investment in their training. The next question might to be ask what they plan to do differently. Informal follow-up questions a couple of weeks later may establish how far the changes are taking effect. It may of course be perfectly obvious to you, without asking questions, that they seem more in control of the work. They may even have said an assertive 'no' to some unreasonable demand that you or others have made; and that might be the most positive indicator of learning having taken place.

Giving feedback

The clearer and more thoughtful the feedback, the greater the chance it will be used. You can test this by thinking about what happens when there is a breakdown in everyday conversation. Nothing is more frustrating than answering a question and then receiving a vague uninformative response from the questioner. You will find yourself wondering, was the question valid? Does the questioner actually know if your answer was appropriate? Have they understood or heard your answer? Is what you said so off-beam that they are bemused by the state of your ignorance? Any or all of these responses may run through your head when you get poor feedback in a conversation. Such negative feelings will abound if you get or give imprecise or unhelpful feedback on a work assignment.

You will remember that in Chapter 2, 'Helping people learn at work', you were given some guidelines on how to make feedback useful. To summarize, if feedback is to be useful, it should be:

- objective and not judgemental;
- specific and illustrated by observed behaviour;
- relevant to the needs of the person being helped;
- relative to behaviour that the recipient has some chance of changing;
- as soon after the event as possible.

The longer after completion of a task feedback is given, the poorer is the chance that we will incorporate some or all of what is said into future practice. You will probably have experienced poor or late response to formal learning activities at school or college. We want to know how we have done, and the sooner the better. The longer the essay or project report remained unmarked in the school staff room, the less interest the marks and comments aroused when you eventually got to read them. Late assessment feedback means that, as a learner, you have to rehearse the experience of doing the work in order to understand why it has been assessed the way it has. You have moved on by this time and your learning objectives are focused in new directions.

Feedback on performance, particularly when it involves learning new knowledge and skills or reviewing and adopting new behaviours, must be timely. As with all types of learning, learning by feedback is entirely a matter of choice for the recipient. They have the right to hear it and learn from it, but you cannot impose your will by forcing someone to accept feedback.

Using staff appraisal to improve learning

Some form of staff appraisal plays a part in the human resource policy and practice of many organizations. If you do not have a staff appraisal scheme, do you know why this is so? Is it that someone in senior management questions the benefits of running a formal scheme? Or it may be that you work in a small or medium-size enterprise where appraisal has yet to be implemented across the organization. There is no doubt that if it is done well it can be a driving force for learning development.

Staff appraisal provides the opportunity to review individual development plans and plan new objectives. It can be a powerful way of reinforcing the message that yours is a learning organization. It can prevent *ad hoc* decisions on staff development. Without a regular review and recording of objectives and development plans there is the risk that some staff get the lion's share of available resources while some slip through the net and never engage in training and development. Also, there is less chance that the organization's mission and business plan will be supported appropriately by training and development, if the enthusiasts are pursuing their own personal training agendas without benefit to the organization.

Most of us need the security of knowing how we are doing at work. We ought to have working relationships which make it possible to discuss openly things which we find difficult or problematic. We also need to be reassured that our achievements are recognized by others for their true quality.

When objectives for the coming year have been defined and agreed with an appraisee, it will often become apparent that there are training needs to be addressed. In some organizations there is a commitment to find resources for any training need which has to be met if the work is to be delivered to standard. There may also be other training needs which the employee and the manager discuss; these may not be in the vital category, but are recorded as desirable if funds permit. As this book has made clear, there are many other opportunities for development within the workplace which do not involve paying out for a course or workshop. If you have managed to develop a learning relationship with your staff, it will be possible to provide quite detailed feedback on aspects of performance and to include in the development plan some work-based training opportunities.

How would you formulate and record the outcomes of this type of appraisal discussion?

An objective and an associated development proposal based on an Internet project might be something like the following.

1 *Objective.* During the next six months to create a company web site and make a proposal on ways in which the Internet may be further exploited.
2 *Development proposal.* To:
   • arrange a study visit to the local university infor-mation services department;
   • identify a range of benchmark companies and use their web sites to see what they are doing;
   • subscribe to relevant web magazines;
   • liaise with the company's marketing consultants;
   • fix coaching session with systems manager;
   • acquire a web authoring package and spend time working through its tutorial;
   • make recommendations on the best way to set up a web site and identify other commercial possibilities in using the Internet.

Within this development proposal there is a variety of activities of the type described in Chapter 7, 'Developing your staff as they work' and Chapter 8, 'Training and development opportunities outside the workplace'.

An effective appraisal scheme will include discussions and informal interviews at key stages during the year. For example, as the manager of the project leader for the Internet development you will want to know how things are pro-gressing at agreed intervals. If you work in a small group, you can have almost daily opportunities to exchange infor-mation and give feedback.

If you want more help in identifying development needs, refer to Chapter 4, 'Learning needs and how to analyse them'.

If you tend to think of training solutions mainly in terms of finding the right course, refer to Chapter 5, 'Choosing training events' and Chapter 6, 'Getting the best out of training events'.

You should also be thinking of other kinds of development activity in or outside the workplace. These were covered in Chapter 7, 'Developing your staff as they work' and Chapter 8, 'Training and development opportunities outside the workplace'. Here is a reminder of the range of activities you may want to discuss with your member of staff:

- in-house training course;
- external course;
- a course leading to an award;
- acting up;
- Action Learning;
- coaching;
- delegation;
- demonstration/instruction;
- mentoring;
- project work;
- work shadowing;
- away days;
- outdoor learning;
- community action;
- secondments;
- study visits, exhibitions and exchanges;
- open learning.

Using peer and upward appraisal to improve learning

Appraisal need not be uni-directional, of course. It is likely that in an appraisal interview you as the manager will be interested to hear usable feedback from your employee. How have you helped or hindered the attainment of objectives? How consistent have you been in applying the standards that have been agreed in previous appraisals? If you are secure in your role you will not find this too challenging. It will probably help your member of staff if you model the type of feedback which is helpful when you discuss their progress. You may also need to show that you are open to comment and not going to become either defensive or aggressive when confronted by feedback which you find difficult to accept. Many managers start by defining the limits within which they are seeking feedback, for example, only on aspects of their management which have directly affected the employee.

The most comprehensive exchange of appraisal information is 360 degree appraisal. Here there is usually a good case for using a facilitator from outside the work group. Organizations which use 360 degree appraisal report that the collection and exchange of information must be handled with care and sensitivity. Such schemes also require a system of documentation to capture and process statements. This allows an external facilitator to identify issues and present findings in ways which people can work on positively. The introduction of this type of appraisal should be a matter of corporate decision.

Nearer home, you as a manager of a work group can use small team meetings and focus groups to manage informal exchanges of peer feedback. There are ways of encouraging a more open level of communication, using the simple checklist of feedback rules referred to above. Maybe you should have them written up on a sheet of flip-chart paper, so that you can invoke them when someone descends to point scoring or destructive opinion giving. Firmly and systematically applying them will enable the group to learn the difference between an unproductive wrangle and a useful exchange of learning points.

Summary

In this chapter you first considered ways of matching assessment methods to different types of learning. We returned to the four-part diagram of the training process and recognized that assessment is to do with measuring how far learning

objectives have been met through the training and development activities that have been provided. It is increasingly the
case that assessment is based on evidence of competence to
do the job; many of the performance improvements that you
will be looking for in your staff can only be fairly measured
in this way.

Once assessments have been made they must be communi-
cated. We returned to the important skill of giving feedback.
The chapter continued with a review of the appraisal process
and you were given an example of objective setting and an
associated development proposal, in this case to set up a
company web site. The value of peer and upward appraisal
was also discussed.

Reading on

Rae, L. (1997), *How to Measure Training Effectiveness*, 3rd edn,
    Aldershot: Gower. (Contains three new chapters on the
    evaluation process and new materials on competence stan-
    dards for training.)

■ 13

Learning development in your work group

The emphasis in this chapter is on the formal aspects of managing learning development. Without some degree of planning at corporate and work-group level, development will become haphazard and detached from the main business needs of the organization. Only you will know at what level you have to take responsibility for setting up and maintaining policy and procedures for learning development. If you work in a small company where no development planning has been done, adapt and use the ideas in this chapter to suit your local situation. You might also decide to seek some help from your local Training and Enterprise Council who may be able to offer you practical guidance and part funding to set up a system.

The aim of this chapter is to equip you to organize the stages of learning development from recruitment to appraisal and set these activities within the context of a learning development policy and annual plan.

To achieve this you will be asked to:

* *review the selection and induction of new staff to ensure they join knowing the value the organization attaches to learning;*
* *assess your staff appraisal scheme to see how it contributes to learning development;*
* *either review your learning development policy and procedures if you have them or start the process of ensuring that they are drafted.*

These are the topics you will be reading more about:

* *selecting new staff;*

- *inducting new staff;*
- *running an effective staff appraisal scheme;*
- *running an effective learning development programme.*

Selecting new staff

Staff selection could be where some of your development initiatives start to go wrong. If you are not selecting and recruiting people who have the necessary competence for the tasks you need doing, you are putting an unnecessary load on any subsequent development programmes you provide. If recruits have not got the personality and the potential that will fit with your work group, you are storing up problems for yourself. It is beyond the scope of this book to cover all the necessary skills that make for good staff selection. However, run through the following checklist. It may prompt you to reassess how you currently select and you might decide to seek further expert help to make the best choices. (Even if you are fortunate enough to have the professional help of a personnel department or an external recruitment consultancy, you should still retain control of the task by giving a very clear job description and person specification as the basis for seeking candidates.)

1   Do you always seek to attract a reasonable field for the number and type of vacancies you have to fill?
2   Do you draw up an accurate job description which gives the main duties and responsibilities of the post, and a person specification which describes the competences and personal qualities sought in the jobholder?
3   Do you use the opportunity of a resignation to review the job to assess whether it is still needed and, if so, does the description need modifying?
4   Do you advertise in appropriate media?
5   How well do you handle the administration of the selection process?
6   Do you use only the interview as a means of selection? (If yes, you are placing too much trust in a selection technique which has been shown to be very subjective; some suggested alternatives are described below).

- Do you give feedback to all candidates, whether successful or not?
- Do you have a comprehensive offer package for the successful candidate or candidates, explaining all the conditions of employment?

This checklist should have enabled you to confirm how well you are managing the process of selecting staff. Here are some suggestions for further improving the process.

In Chapter 7, 'Developing your staff as they work', we talked about the advantages of promoting staff into vacancies after a period of acting up. Remember, too, the warning that you should comply with equal opportunities legislation by putting most posts out to wider competition. Your internal candidate can then measure their performance against that of external candidates.

Consider setting standards for the response time to applications; for example, 'All applicants will receive acknowledgement of their applications within three working days of receipt.'

Consider designing simple exercises which require some demonstration of the skills needed in the job. If particular levels of literacy are important, ask candidates to write a test exercise based on a typical letter or report. Consider the use of psychometric testing for some posts (it is, however, essential that these are professionally administered for you).

Inducting new staff

The early days and weeks in post for a new jobholder provide some important opportunities for you as their manager. You have the opportunity to begin to assess their competence. Once they have settled in, you can draw up an initial set of objectives and do a learning needs analysis; there is guidance on how to do this in Chapter 4, 'Learning needs and how to analyse them'. You also have the opportunity to establish the value you and your colleagues attach to the learning process. Appoint a more experienced colleague to provide information and support to the new member of staff. Although corporate induction days have their place, they should be regarded as a useful organizational ritual rather than a serious opportunity to help the person do the job. Here is a checklist of questions to ask yourself to help ensure that you lay good foundations for a new appointment.

1 Do you have an established 'welcome' procedure for the first day, helping the new appointee to settle in and find their bearings?
2 Do you or your deputy ensure that you personally welcome the new appointee on the first day?
3 Have you drawn up a checklist of personnel, employment and health and safety requirements that need to be explained to the new appointee?
4 Do you always schedule and keep to an arrangement to spend an hour or so with a new appointee during the first week? This will be used to map out initial objectives for the first three months and to identify any training needs that have to be met.
5 Do you always review progress against objectives towards the end of the new appointee's period of probation?

Running an effective staff appraisal scheme

Staff appraisal schemes have been mentioned regularly throughout the book and in particular in Chapter 12, 'Assessing learning outcomes'. If you operate some form of staff appraisal, run through this set of questions and consider how far your scheme contributes to learning development.

1 How well organized is your approach to appraisal? Does it have:
   • a clear rationale within your human resource development policy;
   • published guidelines for appraisers and appraisees;
   • monitoring and appeal arrangements to ensure that judgements are consistent and seen to be fair?
2 Do appraisal interviews happen:
   • on schedule or late;

- at appropriate or inappropriate intervals;
- with sufficient notice and preparation for both parties?
3 Do you review past performance to see how far agreed objectives have been achieved?
4 In planning forward objectives do you:
- identify not more than six;
- make them SMART;
- relate them to agreed standards of performance;
- agree to review them at least half-way through the year or sooner if circumstances change?
5 If your appraisal system leads to performance-related pay awards, do you:
- explain and use agreed criteria for awarding grades;
- distinguish between one-off bonuses for above average performance on a project or special assignment, and additional and consolidated pay awards for sustained excellence in all aspects of the job?
6 Does the appraisal process also identify:
- training and development needs;
- suitable training and development which relate to the attainment of agreed objectives;
- other training and development activities which are desirable in the longer term if resources permit?
7 In general, can you say that appraisal is a positive learning experience:
- for you the appraiser;
- for those you appraise?

Running an effective learning development programme

Just as you would expect to find, in your organization, policies on customer care, health and safety, and equal opportunities, equally you should consider developing and agreeing a policy for training and development, if you do not already have one.

A learning development policy

One important indicator of greater commitment to learning is the drawing up and agreeing of a learning development policy. A policy is a shared and public statement from which procedures can flow. It also usually puts the funding of learning development on a firmer footing – if it is in the policy, there must be a commitment to action and the funds needed to support that action.

You may already have a policy for learning development in your organization, in which case it might be worth reading it through again to see how effectively you are complying with it. Is it an enabling document? Does it have vision?

As a manager in an organization which has no training department or in-house trainers, you may not have adopted a policy yet. You and other managers should consider drafting one. If you have not done this before, seek the help of a training professional or see if you can to look through some policies of other organizations. As a brief guide, you might expect a policy to have the following headings.

1 *The purpose of the policy.* For example: 'This policy states X Ltd's commitment to offering learning development opportunities to our staff. It also defines the crucial role of work-based development activities and requires managers and staff to take joint responsibility for ensuring that the learning derived from them is reinvested in individual and organizational growth . . .'

2 *A definition of learning development.* For example: 'By learning development is meant:
   - all those training activities where learning objectives are planned and their attainment assessed;
   - any work-based activity where individual or organizational learning outcomes are identified, discussed and used for the improvement of performance . . .'

3 *The philosophy.* For example: 'We recognize that learning development is essential for the future growth and competitiveness of the company. We seek to enable staff to plan their own development to meet both their needs and those of the company. We regard development as a

continuous process in the workplace and not one which depends solely on attending courses, important though these may be . . .'

4   *To whom the policy applies.*   For example: 'This policy applies to all employees . . .'

5   *What the employer is committed to do.*   For example: 'It is the responsibility of the senior management team to approve an annual learning development plan . . .'

6   *What individuals are required to do.*   For example: 'All employees are required to participate in a review, with their managers, of their learning development needs at least once a year . . .'

7   *Organizational control.*   For example: 'Learning development priorities are defined centrally by the senior management team at least annually. Departments are expected to produce and cost their own development plans to meet organizational and departmental priorities. They will bid for funds from the centre annually . . .'

8   *Performance measures.*   For example: 'We recognize that some outcomes from learning development activities can be measured only in the medium to long term. However, all formal training will be evaluated and ratings recorded. We will also endeavour to measure performance before and after training inputs, and quantify the performance gains, wherever possible, in terms of cost reduction or increased productivity . . .'

9   *Evaluation and review.*   For example: 'This policy will be reviewed by the senior management team annually . . .'

Learning development procedures

Policies deal with the broad strategies to achieve organizational goals. You will need procedures to make sure that the policy is implemented. These will obviously vary from organization to organization. Below is a checklist of some of the main functions and processes which should be documented.

1   *The planning cycle.*   Do you have an annual timetable for

defining training needs and bidding for funds? Are staff nominated to ensure that the timetable is met?

2 *Funding of training and development.* How are funding decisions made – by a central unit or manager, or are they devolved to departments? (In larger organizations devolution is more common and locates responsibility closer to the production line or service delivery point.)

3 *Record keeping.* Are all training and development activities and outcomes recorded and analysed?

4 *Communications.* How do people know what the policy and procedures are and what training is available?

5 *Administration.* Who is responsible for this and what documents should managers and trainees use?

6 *Evaluation.* What mechanisms (analysis of evaluation forms, sample post-course interviews, focus groups) are used to measure the value of training and development? How often is the training and development system evaluated? Who has responsibility for doing it?

An annual learning development plan

You will need to draw up an annual plan. In a large organization this will be done on a departmental basis. Such a plan should take account of the overall policy for learning development and any priorities that senior management have defined in order to meet the business plan. Collate and analyse the information you have gathered during your individual appraisal interviews so that you can balance company-wide and local objectives. As with most aspects of management decision making, it will be far more motivating for employees if they have some opportunity to take part in this process.

Here is a checklist of headings for a learning development plan.

1 Work-group learning needs assessment – a summary of the main needs in the light of business objectives and level of workforce competence.

2 Key objectives for learning development of the work

group (showing the connection with the corporate and work-group business plans).

3 Methods, showing choice of learning activities.
4 Sourcing of training, showing internal and external providers.
5 Budget.
6 Evaluation, showing methods for measuring performance improvement wherever possible.

Summary

In this chapter we have looked at how you can plan to meet the learning development needs of your work group on a systematic basis. In particular, you were asked to consider what you are doing to meet the development needs of your staff at all stages of their employment in the organization, starting with the selection and induction of new staff and following on to appraisal. You then considered what kind of learning development policies and procedures you need. You concluded by noting some elements of an annual plan.

If you work in a larger company some of these planning functions may already have been tackled by training managers. However, as a manager of a work group you still have an important role in making sure that policies are carried through.

Reading on

Pepper, A. (1992), *Managing the Training and Development Function*, 2nd edn, Aldershot: Gower. (This book will give you further guidance on writing policies and procedures which are in line with your organization's business goals.)

■ 14

Learning for change

As you were reading this book you may have been aware that some of the ideas and suggestions presented are already in use in your organization. There may have been others which are very new to you or, if not new, still to be adopted. For example, not all organizations have staff appraisal schemes. Whilst there may be historical reasons in your workplace why you have not got one, it would be hard to resist the argument that there must be some form of performance measurement and management in any successful organization. This final chapter will help you decide where your organization stands in the journey towards becoming more of a learning organization.

The aim of this chapter is to help you:

- assess the broad strategy for learning development in your organization;
- focus on ways of achieving progress in planning individual, group and personal development.

To achieve this you will be asked to:

- read five short descriptions of companies at different stages in the process of integrating learning development;
- determine where your own organization stands;
- consider three aspects of managing change;
- reflect on how you communicate the changes you wish to achieve.

These are the topics you will be reading more about:

- learning development throughout your organization;
- managing change.

Learning development throughout your organization

Where does your organization currently stand with regard to learning development?

Read the following descriptions of companies with differing levels of commitment to learning development and judge which most closely approximates to that of your own organization.

1   *No organized training and development.* This company has no separate human resource development (HRD) specialist and has yet to develop a learning development policy. What little learning activity that occurs is either in the form of work-based coaching or is chosen on impulse by senior staff wanting to attend the odd external course.

2   *Occasional training to meet demands, but no formal training policy.* In this organization there is an awareness of the importance of training if it is to remain competitive. However, training is often planned after the shortfall in skills has already begun to hamper production. (This is one aspect of a general scenario of crisis management.) Because learning development does not operate within the bounds of an agreed policy, no formal budget is allocated and it is therefore necessary to fight for funds whenever a training need is defined.

3   *Training based on a policy produced for the organization by Personnel/HRD.* In this company there is a an appointed training specialist within the personnel department. He or she has conducted a detailed training needs analysis in the main functional areas and has prepared a corporate training and development policy for the board. This has been approved and funds have been designated to provide a range of training support, much of which is to be delivered in-house.

4   *A comprehensive learning development programme, based on training needs defined by departments.* In this organization learning development is planned as a consequence of

annual staff appraisal interviews. Line managers work in conjunction with HRD specialists. The training and development policy is drawn up by senior managers, including HRD specialists. On a day-to-day basis, training needs are assessed by line managers and responded to by work-based coaching and instruction.

5 *Organization-wide learning development initiatives built in at all levels as part of the business plan.* In this company learning development is seen as a means of supporting operations, defining future products and services, and enabling strategic development. The HRD specialists operate as internal consultants to line managers and the senior management team. There is a wide commitment to planning and resourcing learning development into all initiatives. The majority of managers would not question that developing their staff was one of their prime responsibilities. The company runs a learning development centre, which makes learning programmes available to all staff. It is restructuring itself to exploit more fully the potential of all staff to grow into new roles and contribute to business development. The majority of staff would say that working for this organization has given them new opportunities to learn and develop.

Consider which of these organizational types most closely resembles yours. If you are like number 1, you probably are a small to medium-sized organization. You may have grown rapidly because of the entrepreneurial flair of one or two individuals. Now more and more of the key business functions are being allocated to specialist staff. As yet no HRD specialism is available in-house. You may need to seek guidance and possible funding from your local Business Link or an HRD consultancy which you have selected. One of the prime aims of development will be to spread the ideas and approaches outlined in this book so that managers build skill and confidence in their role as developers of their staff.

If you chose number 2, you will need to influence your colleagues in key management positions so that they adopt a more proactive stance towards planning everything, including learning development. This is no small challenge, and again you will benefit from some external input from experts who can help you adopt a more strategic view of the business.

If you are in the position of a number 3 type organization you have jumped some of the organizational hurdles but now need to be wary of assigning all the staff development responsibility to the experts, who will either buckle under the strain or set modest targets so that they cannot fail. There is no doubt, though, that the process of discussing and agreeing a formal policy and allocating a budget for training and development will provide a strong foundation for more radical implementation of learning development throughout the company.

If yours is a number 4 type organization you should find strong support for the approaches outlined in this book. All the main elements are in place and the pay-offs of effective training and development will be evident to all managers.

In a number 5 type company there will have been sustained experience of the benefits of learning development, but something more radical will have happened. The mission statement will have defined in a clear and dynamic way where the company aims to move. There will be a widespread understanding that without a total commitment to quality and meeting customer needs, the business will not grow. It will also be clear that in order to develop new services and products the creative energies of the organization need to be mobilized and rewarded.

Old structures which prevent rapid communication of feedback from customers will have been swept away. The distance between senior managers and the workforce will have been reduced. There will be a preparedness to experiment with new team working. All these processes will be seen as learning opportunities and will be adequately supported by essential learning resources, both through the line manager and the HRD specialist.

If you work in an organization like this, there may be times when you find the rate of change alarming; but you will certainly be learning in a way that no other previous job has made possible. If you do not see this happening at present in your organization, it would be fair to admit that this type of commitment to learning is what many of us aspire to but have yet to reach in our work. It helps to know where you are aiming to go.

Managing change

You may recognize where you are in the stages of organizational development described in the previous section, but how do you move from one stage in the journey to the next? There is no universal formula for doing this; much will depend on the culture and health of your organization as well as your own experience and conviction of the need for change. The best way ahead is to empower managers so that they in turn empower their staff. The basic message of this book is that once managers realize that they are also developers and acquire the necessary skills and confidence, they can help build the systems and processes that your organization needs.

Bite-sized chunks

It is usually a good idea to pilot ideas before going 'live' in too public a way. This avoids the possibility of employees seeing your plans to adopt a more systematic approach to learning and development as another flash in the pan. Develop your own confidence and experience first by working with a small group of staff. You may also consider forming a project group to review current practice and make recommendations for change.

Establishing a learning relationship with individual employees is a good way to start the change process. This individual approach fits in with the concept of 'bite-sized chunks'. You cannot change the world in a day or a hundred days, but you can progressively provide individual learning support to members of your staff and this will help shift the learning environment you all work in. The message will get round that you are accessible and prepared to help. In working with individuals you are also providing that essential and continuing support which trainers are rarely able to give because of the transitory nature of their input.

If this type of relationship has so far been unfamiliar to you, you should gain considerable insights and confidence from working in this way. You might use it to start shifting from a situation where learning development needs are rarely assessed towards a more systematic method based on agreed policy.

Develop a common vision

Most important organizational objectives for change are achieved by having a clear vision which people can support. Such a vision must be brief and readily understandable and, above all, inspirational. Visions may originate in the minds of managers, but if they are to make any difference, they have to be shared intellectually and emotionally by all employees. If you want to create an environment at work which is supportive of learning you might consider creating a vision or message with which everyone can identify. Consider using some time during a team meeting to try to formulate a statement which encapsulates what you aim to achieve as a learning organization or work group.

Ask members what type of organization they want to work in with reference to the following issues (you might choose to divide the whole group into sub-groups and ask them to take three or four issues each):

• acknowledging and learning from mistakes and successes;
• developing and valuing systems for giving and receiving useful feedback and appraisal;
• taking stock regularly of how work assignments have been achieved to see what can be improved;
• seeking improvement suggestions;
• giving greater responsibility down the line;
• identifying learning needs;

- seeking solutions to learning needs first within the work group;
- making sure that investment in learning development pays off in terms of improved performance;
- rewarding creativity and progress in learning.

Bring the sub-groups back together to share ideas. Try to combine the most important statements that have been generated into a short paragraph which says where you aim to be. At subsequent meetings consider each issue and discuss what systems you need to set up to ensure that your vision progressively becomes a reality.

Take account of the larger environment

Remember that, whatever your position in the management hierarchy, you are part of a larger organizational system. In developing your work group, there is always the risk of becoming out of step with the approaches and priorities of the organization as a whole.

One way to progress without exposing yourself to too many risks of organizational skirmishing or ambush is to communicate widely. This means listening to and talking with:

- your work group;
- your own line manager;
- your internal and external customers.

Communicate with your work group

Use regular team briefings to share your plans and draw on the inventiveness and the commitment of the group. Expect resistance from some individuals. You cannot change without some nervous individuals holding on to old ways. Support the behaviours that will make for greater openness and involvement. When your staff achieve through learning, publicize it widely.

Communicate with your own line manager

Keep your line manager fully in the picture. Few managers do not want to be associated with success. When, by developing your staff, you deliver better results, this will speak powerfully in favour of your approaches. In some cases your manager may even appropriate your success. Annoying though this might be, it does at least mean that your manager will find it difficult not to support further developments. More likely, you will have a better relationship with your manager and can gain much valuable feedback and support as you plan to encourage your work group to greater commitment to learn.

Communicate with your internal and external customers

If you lose touch with the needs and responses of either internal or external customers or, worse still, both, you will not have the strength to achieve change. As you improve the skills and knowledge of your work group, this must be manifest in improved products or services. Telling your customers about the ways you are planning to improve performance helps embed the changes with your staff. Obtaining and passing on feedback when people have noticed improvements further consolidates growth.

Communicate with your mentor

Another strategy for introducing a fresh approach to learning and development in your work group is to identify for yourself a mentor within or outside the organization. You may remember that this was suggested in the first chapter of this book.

Choose someone who has already created a learning environment for their own work group. They may or may not work in your organization. Talk over your plans for introducing performance appraisal or discuss with them your plans for a training event which you plan to commission or run. If you are struggling to find ways of improving the performance of a resistant individual, this too can be discussed. Implement whatever approach you decide on and then review with your mentor how the individual's behaviour has changed.

Summary

In this final chapter you have identified where your organization stands with regard to five stages in the growth of good practice in learning development. The examples you were given ranged from a company with no in-house expertise and no systematic policy or practice in learning development to one where a well-established policy is implemented widely by senior and line managers as well as by staff.

You also considered some change management issues. Better to bite off what you can chew and work at changing day-to-day learning relationships. Developing a common vision is essential if you are to gain commitment from your staff. You were given a checklist to use in a discussion on the theme, 'What type of organization do you want to work in?'

Taking account of the larger organization in which you work, it was suggested that you communicate regularly and effectively with:

- your work group;
- your own line manager;
- your internal and external customers.

Reading on

Jones, S. (1996), *Developing a Learning Culture*, Maidenhead: McGraw-Hill. (This book is strong on the value of team work in implementing change strategies; there are also useful examples drawn from businesses of all sizes.)

Your learning development planner

This final section of the book comprises a planner to help you decide what action to take to ensure that your work group realizes the benefits of becoming more of a learning organization. In making these plans you will be able to draw on the methods and techniques you have read about throughout the book.

The short section, 'Action planning for learning development', which follows is designed to help start discussions with your mentor. Complete the activity and use it as the basis for your first meeting.

Analyse how well you as a manager enable people to learn

Consider what steps you should take to improve your effectiveness as a manager who helps people learn. Start by completing a SWOT (Strengths, Weaknesses, Opportunities, Threats) analysis on page 215, using the instructions below.

Use the four boxes to make a list of your strengths and weaknesses as a staff developer, the opportunities for development which you see in your workplace and the threats that might reduce your scope for action.

For example, under 'Strengths' you might list that you run an effective staff appraisal scheme and that it does genuinely contribute to performance improvement and the identification of learning needs. You might mention that you have developed skills in giving and receiving feedback or have set up coaching for an individual. List all the learning development skills and activities you regard as your strengths.

Under 'Weaknesses' you should list those aspects of your current performance as a staff developer which you need to improve. For example, reading this book may have made you realize that you are not grasping all the opportunities for helping people learn as they work; or you may not have given much attention to sending people on workshops and courses.

In the two lower boxes, assess the opportunities for positive development, and the threats that face you in seizing them. For example, under 'Opportunities' you may list some reorganization of staffing or management which will give you greater scope. It may be that there is a new manager above you who can give you real support or you have identified a member of your own staff who understands what you are aiming to do.

There is not usually a shortage of threats to change. The most likely is lack of funds, but this may be less of an obstacle if you explore all the opportunities for learning available to you within the organization.

Be as honest as you can; you may choose to write your responses on a separate sheet of paper.

SWOT Analysis

Strengths	Weaknesses
Opportunities	Threats

Action planning for learning development

When you have filled in the SWOT analysis boxes, think about the following questions and then complete and write down the sentences which follow.

1 Can you think of any way in which your strengths as a manager who encourages learning could be further developed? What would this involve?

   • *I would like to develop my strengths by . . .*

2 Think of your weaknesses as a staff developer. Can you suggest ways of overcoming them?

   • *Some ways of overcoming weaknesses would be . . .*

3 Review the opportunities you have to create an improved learning environment for yourself and your people; how do you propose to go about grasping them?

   • *I plan to . . .*

4 If you see no opportunities at present, what opportunities
   would you like there to be and what might make them
   more realizable?

   • *I would like to . . .*

   • *I will take the following action to make these opportunities
     more realizable . . .*

5 If you are in a situation which you perceive as inhospitable
   to learning development, how could you go about
   removing or reducing the threat?

   • *I would like to . . .*

# Conclusion

You may remember that in the opening chapters of this book the point was made very clearly that no one can learn for somebody else. Your own development is your responsibility. Of course you should have access to all kinds of help from your staff, your peers and your own manager. Your chosen development plan may include formal study for a qualification or a planned series of short courses designed to fill skills and knowledge gaps. Open learning may offer another avenue to explore in your development. You may have decided to find yourself a mentor who can give you a friendly ear and feedback on some of the issues which face you in your job. You may have decided to use the development opportunities that present themselves as part of your staff appraisal process. Agreeing objectives and appropriate development activities in discussion with your own manager may enhance mutual understanding and make for more effective collaboration between you. It may be that you have outgrown the development possibilities in your present job and now need to plan a career move.

The other important theme to which we return at the end of this book is that helping people learn offers you the chance to learn and develop your management skills. The personal satisfaction of seeing your staff overcome problems and extend and improve their performance is in itself a reward which makes up for some of the more arduous aspects of the manager's role and responsibilities.

Index